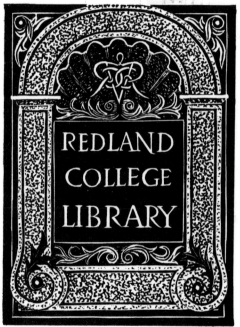

REDLAND
COLLEGE
LIBRARY

THE HOME AND THE SCHOOL

STUDIES IN SOCIETY

General Editors: Ruth and David Glass

Already published

Lewis W. Jones

COLD REBELLION: The South's Oligarchy in Revolt

Bernard Semmel

THE GOVERNOR EYRE CONTROVERSY

W. L. Guttsman

THE BRITISH POLITICAL ELITE

Vittorio Lanternari

THE RELIGIONS OF THE OPPRESSED

———

Other books about this study

★

MATERNITY IN GREAT BRITAIN

Oxford University Press: 1948

CHILDREN UNDER FIVE

Allen and Unwin: 1958

J. W. B. DOUGLAS

Director of the Medical Research Council Unit at the
London School of Economics

The Home and the School

A STUDY OF ABILITY AND ATTAINMENT
IN THE PRIMARY SCHOOL

*

With an Introduction by

Professor D. V. Glass

Chairman
Population Investigation Committee

LONDON
MACGIBBON & KEE
MCMLXIX

FIRST PUBLISHED 1964 BY MACGIBBON AND KEE LTD
3 UPPER JAMES STREET, GOLDEN SQUARE, LONDON W1
SECOND IMPRESSION APRIL 1964
THIRD IMPRESSION NOVEMBER 1964
FOURTH IMPRESSION JANUARY 1966
FIFTH IMPRESSION NOVEMBER 1966
SIXTH IMPRESSION MARCH 1968
SEVENTH IMPRESSION JULY 1969
COPYRIGHT © J. W. B. DOUGLAS 1964

SBN 261 61642 0

PRINTED IN GREAT BRITAIN BY
EBENEZER BAYLIS AND SON LTD
WORCESTER AND LONDON

*To the Mothers and Children
who by their generous help have made
this study possible*

ACKNOWLEDGEMENTS

THIS study owes its success to the generous help given by Directors of Education, Medical Officers of Health, Teachers, School Doctors and School Nurses throughout the country. In recent years it has been supported by grants from the Nuffield Foundation, the Population Council (Inc.) and the Medical Research Council, and accommodation has been provided by the Department of Public Health and Social Medicine of the University of Edinburgh and, more recently, by the London School of Economics.

Mrs James Clow, who as Miss J. M. Blomfield collaborated with me in *Children Under Five*, was responsible for much of the early work on this material. Miss Jean Ross who is currently working on the secondary school progress of these children, gave me much help in preparing the final draft of this report. The tests used in the report are described on page 129 by D. A. Pidgeon of the National Foundation for Educational Research (in England and Wales) who has given me constant help and advice. H. R. Simpson of Rothamsted Experimental Station devised and carried out the statistical analysis described on page 133.

I have throughout enjoyed the advice of the individual members of the survey committee and in particular of Professor D. V. Glass and Dr W. D. Wall. Among others who have helped at various stages are John Nimmo, Mrs G. M. Cleary, Miss E. Ellis, and Miss P. Heneghan of the Department of Public Health and Social Medicine of the University of Edinburgh, and I. W. Henry, Miss C. Brewer and Miss O. Petty of this Medical Research Council Unit.

J.W.B.D.

CONTENTS

INTRODUCTION

D. V. GLASS

Chairman
Population Investigation Committee

———

THIS study of children in the primary school years is the third main report on a follow-up investigation initiated by, and carried out under the auspices of, the Population Investigation Committee.[1] The investigation, directed by Dr J. W. B. Douglas since it began in 1945, was originally undertaken to examine the availability and effectiveness of the ante-natal and maternity services in Britain, drawing upon the actual experience of a representative sample of mothers as the main source of information. The Royal Commission on Population was taking evidence at the time, and one of the purposes of the inquiry was to provide material for that Commission. But since the new National Health Service was about to be launched, it was also hoped that the results of the inquiry would provide yardstick data against which the changes brought about by the new system could be studied later by the government or by some independent research organisation.[2]

The initial investigation, carried out in 1946, was highly successful. Almost every Medical Officer of Health in Britain co-operated, allowing us to use the Health Visitors as unpaid interviewers. The mothers covered by the survey—the inquiry was based upon interviews with every woman in Britain

[1] The two earlier volumes are: Joint Committee of R.C.O.G. and Population Investigation Committee, *Maternity in Great Britain*, London, 1948 (the volume was written by J. W. B. Douglas and G. Rowntree); and J. W. B. Douglas and J. M. Bloomfield, *Children under Five*, London, 1958. In addition more than thirty papers have been published by Dr Douglas and his colleagues on special aspects of the survey results.

[2] The National Birthday Trust Fund included in their recent study of perinatal and infant mortality, a number of questions which will allow an assessment of changes in some aspects of the ante-natal and maternity services since 1946.

who had borne a child in one week in March, 1946—were no less helpful. Very few refused to co-operate, and the information they gave was wide-ranging and relevant. *Maternity in Great Britain*[1] was to a large extent derived from an analysis of their answers to the interview questionnaires.

It had not originally been intended to continue the research beyond the 1946 study. But the potential value of a follow-up study was so evident, that a superb opportunity would have been missed if some institution had not attempted to keep in touch with the children and their families, recording their experience in respect of problems of health and growth, of educational development and social change. It was for this reason that the Population Investigation Committee decided to continue the study as part of its own research programme.

Since 1946 the resultant follow-up study has been financed very largely by grants from foundations—especially from the Nuffield and Ford Foundations and from the Population Council, Inc. Government grants in support of the research were not available until very recently, and then only for special aspects of the work. Funds were often short.[2] But they were supplemented by very substantial assistance in kind, given especially by the Medical Officers of Health and the School Medical Service; and also by the generous collaboration of the National Foundation for Educational Research, the Rothamsted Experimental Station and various government departments. In particular, the enormous volume of basic interviewing (for the children and their parents have been

---

[1] In addition, there were detailed case studies of a number of areas, illustrative of the range of provision of services.

[2] We have also received grants from the Hospital for Sick Children, Great Ormond Street; from 14 Regional Hospital Boards; the National Birthday Trust Fund; the National Spastics Society and the Medical Research Council. And we are indebted to the University of Edinburgh for much help during the period when Dr Douglas was the Reader in Public Health and Social Medicine there. In general, however, though follow-up studies are among the most valuable vehicles for social research, they are the most difficult to finance. Foundations prefer to be pioneers. Once a follow-up study is a 'going concern', it becomes very difficult to obtain further support from Foundations.

interviewed many times since 1946) has been provided free of charge. It is to this unpaid interviewing, carried out enthusiastically by Health Visitors and School Nurses; to the help of the Directors of Education and the teachers in administering various tests and in supplying a vast amount of information; and to the co-operation of the five thousand families concerned, that we owe the success of what up to the present is a unique example of a study which has followed a representative population of children from birth.[1]

The children in the study are now almost eighteen years of age. We are still in touch with them, following them into work or into higher education. The continued investigation of the group now forms part of the programme of a Medical Research Council Unit, established at the London School of Economics, and most appropriately under the direction of Dr Douglas.

During the eighteen years of study, the focus of the investigation has naturally changed very considerably. At first concerned with the quantity and quality of ante-natal and maternity services, the early stages of the follow-up concentrated upon major types of illness suffered by the children up to the age of five. The next stage, the results of which are reported upon in the present book, paid particular attention to primary education. Subsequently, the children's progress in the secondary school system was the main interest and the analysis of that progress will be the subject of the next volume. The children—they are young adults now—have since been followed from school into employment, and the transition from school to work or higher education will be examined in yet another volume.

[1] The other major follow-up study of a representative sample of children is that being undertaken by the Scottish Council for Research in Education, and derives from the 1947 inquiry, initiated jointly by the Council and by the Population Investigation Committee, into the trend of intelligence. (*See* J. S. MacPherson, *Eleven-year-olds grow up*, London, 1958.) But that study began with children aged 11 years. The well-known studies by the late Lewis Terman and his colleagues in California represent the most extensive (in time) investigation but deal exclusively with a sample of 'gifted' children, predominantly with I.Q.'s of 135 and over. (*See* L. M. Terman and M. H. Oden, *The gifted group at mid-life*, Stanford, 1959.)

Throughout the inquiry, the changing specific studies have been linked by a continuing interest in the influence of the environment upon health, development and achievement. But this in turn has also involved the study of individual and group differences in attitudes and behaviour and also the need to assess the extent to which such differences between groups of parents account for the major features of the differences between the children. For example, in examining the factors affecting illness among children during the first year of life, we were concerned to know whether differences in the quality of 'maternal care' played an important part in the differing incidence of lower respiratory infections between the social classes, and it was clear that they did. But it was equally clear that the influence of maternal care was most powerful when housing conditions were good; in poor housing conditions even the most conscientious mothers could do relatively little. Similarly, in the primary school years there was a strong association between measured intelligence, school performance and success at the '11+' examination. But the study has shown how, even within the narrow span of years between 8 and 11, measured intelligence responds to environmental factors (including the family environment) and also how, especially in the border zone of 110–120 I.Q., environmental factors affect the allocation of children to grammar or secondary modern schools. These environmental effects demand a critical reappraisal with respect to the question of which aspects are most significant for which groups of children and at what stages in their development. Some of the more powerful aspects of the environment include the condition of the home; the degree of parental encouragement given to the children; the previous academic record of the primary schools (that is, the proportion of their pupils reaching grammar schools); and the 'streams' in which children are placed early in their primary school years. But the relevance of the factors differs with social class and with the age of the children. Housing conditions act cumulatively over time on working class children; for middle class children, however, some adjustment appears to be reached as they grow older. The academic record of schools acts differently at different levels.

Schools with a very good academic record show a continued high success rate even if children receive little parental encouragement; while when there is a poor record, even the children who receive much parental encouragement still do badly.[1] But in the entry to primary schools, a much larger proportion of middle class than working class children attended schools with good records, while at the same time a larger proportion of middle class parents gave strong encouragement to their children. For middle class children, therefore, school and family environment tended to reinforce each other positively, for working class children negatively. The 'streaming' of children tended to work in a comparably differential manner.

These examples have been given not to display the positive findings of this inquiry—though they *are* some of its findings —but to illustrate the way in which the environmental factors have been examined. The data needed could not have been collected save by means of a follow-up study; most of them had to be gathered at particular points in the lives of the children and from many sources. In addition, in a follow-up study it is possible, in going back to the participants, to collect further information which current analysis suggests is needed, provided that the information is not distorted by faulty memory. Further, the analysis of new data may suggest that information collected at an earlier stage needs classifying in a different way. To take one instance, during the primary school stage of the inquiry it became clear that the social status classification of the families which had originally been adopted was unsatisfactory. It was not sufficiently stable— families changed their position in the classification too frequently—and its use produced results which sometimes

---

[1] The National Union of Teachers, in the report on its 1962 national survey of schools, inquired into many relevant aspects of primary school conditions (including staff turnover), but not into their record of 'success' at the 11 + examination. (The information collected on the social-class catchment areas of the schools might appear to be of value, but I am doubtful of the reliability of assessments which are based on the simple replies by head teachers to the question: 'How would you describe (socially) the people who live in your catchment area?') *See* N.U.T. *The state of our schools*, Parts 1 and 2, London, 1963.

appeared unwarrantably inconsistent.[1] A new classification was developed by Dr Douglas—using information which had not originally been included in the study—based upon the social origins and education of both the fathers and mothers of the children. In turn this new classification produced a far more coherent picture of parents' aspirations for their children and of differences in the school performance of the children themselves. More consistent patterns over time were also revealed—drawing attention, for example, to those mothers who, in relation to their children in the study, had shown high standards of infant care and management, effective use of the medical services, and marked interest in their children's school performance and prospects. It is above all by this grouping together of successive stages of experience in an effort to see how far, and in respect of what kinds of problems, there are long-run patterns of behaviour linked to subsequent developments, that a long-term follow-up investigation contributes most to research. The approach applies not only to the general study of educational selection and achievement but also to the more specialised inquiries on which Dr Douglas and his colleagues are engaged. One of these inquiries is concerned with ascertaining how far children with histories of disturbed behaviour and emotional maladjustment become juvenile or adolescent delinquents, and—no less important— in what circumstances delinquency does not follow such histories. Another special inquiry is examining the incidence and effectiveness of birth control practice among married couples, looking at the practice not only from the point of view of the customary social class and religious differences but also to see how far the desire for and achievement of a small family have been paralleled by 'planning' in other spheres— in the use of the available medical and social services, in the drive for personal social mobility, in the aspirations for one's

---

[1] The initial social status classification adopted was that which Professor E. Grebenik and I had devised for the 1946 Family Census. This was based primarily upon husband's occupation, though it also took into account the number of employees (in the case of employers or independent workers) and the receipt of a salary or a wage. The circumstances and the scale of the Family Census made it necessary greatly to restrict the number of questions asked.

children. Both these special inquiries are based upon the population covered by the follow-up study, and draw upon information on attitudes and behaviour over a long period of time. And in both cases there is the advantage of being able to compare the experience of particular groups with that of the total population from which the groups are drawn.[1]

But to return to the present book. It is in many respects a pioneer study, and not least in that it is one of the few to examine the response of a large representative sample of children during the early stages of their formal education. Since World War II there has been a considerable increase in educational research in Britain. But much of the research—especially research by sociologists—has been directed towards the later stages of education. This is understandable, for inter-war discussion was heavily concerned with the inadequacy and inequalities of secondary school provision. With the 1944 Act, emphasis shifted to the question of how seemingly objective selection practices distributed children within the framework of what was described as 'secondary education for all', as well as to the level of performance and degree of wastage within the secondary system. Later, with the evidence of a continuing low intake into our universities—not more than about four per cent of the age group entering those institutions in Britain—the problem of university expansion claimed

---

[1] It is essential to be able to ascertain in, say, studying delinquency, not only whether delinquents are predominantly individuals who have shown clusters of behavioural problems, but also the frequency of such clusters among individuals who have not become delinquents. It may be the case, for example, that most delinquents come from broken homes. But it does not follow that most children from broken homes become delinquents. And if they do not, then broken homes cannot be regarded as the primary explanation of delinquency. It is therefore most important to study not only the special group of immediate concern but also the parent population from which it is drawn and (in the case of delinquents, for example) to search for counterbalancing forces in the non-delinquents and reinforcing factors in the delinquents.

Other special analyses based upon the follow-up investigation include a study of children separated temporarily or permanently from their fathers or mothers (or both); the internal migration of families; changes in housing conditions over time; and the growth and behaviour of prematurely born children.

a larger share of interest. And some of the new universities are now flourishing the banners of research into teaching methods and into the relationship between 'town and gown'. That universities are now studying themselves is certainly to be commended. But it is striking and saddening that the funds which such universities are proposing to spend on self-research are considerably larger than any which had formerly been given for studying the base of the educational pyramid. It is equally striking and saddening that at no time had there been an attempt at a thorough study of the educational system as a whole, in spite of the fact that what happens at the base of the pyramid must clearly influence what is practicable at the apex, and that decisions taken about what degree of university expansion should be promoted must entail consequential changes in the nature of primary and secondary education.

How much and what kinds of change, are suggested by the results of Dr Douglas's investigation. To put the main findings as briefly as possible, they show a set of relationships which parallel what was found in an earlier study of social mobility in Britain.[1] That is, though there has been very considerable public action, there is an interlocking network of inequalities, many in spite of that public action, though some because of it. The expansion of educational provision since the 1944 Act has undoubtedly done much to improve the situation as compared with the inter-war years. But many basic inequalities are still only too visible.

Taking the public system in England and Wales, there are first the regional differences in the provision of grammar school places. No differences in the distribution of measured intelligence could possibly justify the range of variation between Wales, with grammar school places provided for twenty-nine per cent of children, and the South, with the provision at only thirteen per cent. The smaller the provision, the smaller the proportionate share of working class children in what is available; middle class children suffer less, quite apart from the fact that they also have access to private education. And

[1] See D. V. Glass et al, Social Mobility in Britain, London, 1954, pp. 16–21.

within the public primary system, there are still major differences in provisions and differences in the use made of the school opportunities, not as a result of conscious educational policy but because of the nature of our society and of the absence of sufficient informed and persistent action to compensate for built-in inequalities of conditions, attitudes and behaviour. Some of the main inequalities have already been mentioned. They tend to work together, and in a negative manner so far as working class children are concerned.

Beginning with handicaps, in the sense of having a poorer physical and cultural environment, the children suffer an intensification of disadvantages, relative to middle class children, during their primary school years. If they live in poor housing conditions, they may well attend schools with a low record of success at the 11+ examination.[1] Those who are least well cared for may find themselves allocated to the lower streams at school and their school performance will tend to conform accordingly. In general they are less likely to receive encouragement from their parents. Between the ages of 8 and 11 years, the working class and middle class children will thus tend to grow further apart in operational ability. If, based on their tests at the age of 8 years, they had had, at each level of measured intelligence the same chances of being awarded a grammar school place as the children of the upper sections of the middle classes, we should have needed fifty-six per cent more grammar school places than were actually available.[2] The gap between the hypothetical and the actual is an indication not only of the continued existence of cumulative inequalities but also of the extent to which our society has

---

[1] In the nineteenth century, the Newcastle Commission argued that 'a set of good schools civilises a whole neighbourhood'. It might almost appear that at present the process is the reverse, a good neighbourhood 'civilising' a whole school.

[2] This analysis applies only to 'success' in the public system. If we take into account the chances, for given levels of measured intelligence at the age of 8 years, of children of the upper middle classes entering all forms of selective secondary education (including the independent schools) then we should need to increase the allotment of grammar school places by 75 per cent. The private system of secondary education helps to give positive reinforcement in favour of middle class children.

failed to encourage the development and realisation of ability at various levels. If we accept Morant's simple definition of the aim of primary education as to 'make the best use of the school years available', we are still far short of that target.[1]

This is all the more serious in that the secondary school system does not compensate for the deficiencies of the primary school years. How could it? Much of the damage done may be irremediable. In any case, secondary schools show little flexibility as regards the transfer of pupils.[2] Only a very small proportion of pupils move from secondary modern to grammar schools (2.0 per cent in the present study) and transfers are more frequent among middle class than among working class children. And though secondary modern schools now provide facilities for older pupils, most of them still leave at the age of 15 years. Among the children in the survey—they reached the age of 15 in 1961—70 per cent of those in secondary modern schools left school at the miminum age, as compared with only 4 per cent of the children in grammar schools. For the large majority of children in secondary modern schools, the minimum school-leaving age marked the end of full-time formal education. Not only does this involve some loss of pupils with high measured ability—for early leaving from the secondary modern schools did not by any means fall exclusively on the least able ranges of children—but, in addition, it leaves the largest proportion of children least prepared for

[1] In order to avoid any misunderstanding, I should like to stress two points. First, for given levels of measured intelligence, working-class children, if they have good housing conditions, attend schools with high success records, and receive substantial parental encouragement, respond in the same way as middle class children. Secondly, the implications of the analysis are that the inequalities of the situation should be removed, *not* by depriving middle class children of a helpful environment, but by providing a comparable environmental stimulus for working class children.

[2] Lord James has said: 'One feels that a lot of what was said on this subject [on our secondary education system] arises out of complete ignorance of what a secondary modern school is like. There isn't anything like this hard and sharp division. The edges are blurred—the boy can transfer from the secondary modern school to the secondary grammar school at 12 or 13, or 15, and is increasingly doing so.' (The *Listener*, July 26th, 1962, p. 124.) Our survey does not support Lord James's optimism.

the world of employment and for the responsibilities of citizenship. In some degree, while we set up committees of inquiry to deal with teenage problems, we may well be encouraging such problems by abandoning those children who most need some form of further, full-time education.[1]

The present system of public primary and secondary education is based upon assumptions which, even when they appear to be realistic, give that appearance because the selection mechanisms used act as self-fulfilling prophecies. But even within their own narrow terms, the mechanisms are imperfect. They select out; but they by no means succeed in keeping in, for subsequent entry to higher education, the top layers of measured intelligence. Around 20 per cent of boys and girls have I.Q.'s of 113 and over. But by June 1962, when the survey children were just above sixteen years of age, fifteen per cent of that highly intelligent group of boys and girls had already given up full-time education, almost four-fifths of the leavers being working class children.[2] And there will no doubt be a further flaking away of the group before the age of university entry is reached. Any proposals for a major expansion of university education would need to take those losses into account and try to prevent them from occurring.

[1] There are now many voices in the U.S.A. pronouncing in favour of an 'elite education' analogous to own. One of the clearest has been that of Admiral Rickover, whose views have been paraphrased by an American superintendent of schools as . . . 'train the best and shoot the rest'. (G. Gallup and E. Hill, 'Is European education better than ours?' *Saturday Evening Post*, December 24th and 31st, 1960.) One might perhaps almost understand that point of view; at least the question of what to do with 'the rest' would be given a definite and final answer. But in our public system we provide no such sharp answer. Instead, we help to create the long term problems which are bound to arise when 'inferior' education is regarded as sufficient for the unfortunate eighty per cent of children, an attitude which, presumably, derives from the assumption that better teachers are required to teach the more able than the less able children. I should add, *à propos* of this discussion, that British sociologists have sometimes been accused of being obsessed with the underprivileged. But I regard the eighty per cent of children in secondary modern schools as 'underprivileged'; and in the circumstances I am prepared to be viewed as 'obsessed'.

[2] Even among boys and girls with I.Q.'s of 120 and over (constituting about the top eight per cent of the I.Q. distribution), more than six per cent had given up full-time education by June 1962.

To do this means that a programme for higher education must not only define and justify its particular targets, but also consider what consequential action needs to be taken at the secondary and primary levels to ensure that the targets are likely to be met.

What should those targets be? Accepting the fact that some of our secondary schools perform functions fulfilled by universities in, say, Canada or the U.S.A., I cannot imagine any reasonable definition of the role of higher education in our society which would justify restricting such education to around four or five per cent of an age group. Even setting the lower limits of entry at I.Q.'s of 120 and over would double that proportion. And that itself is unnecessarily restrictive in comparison either with what is being done in many other societies or with the probable capacity of young men and women to profit from broadly interpreted higher education. Thus if the targets were set at 18 to 20 per cent of the age group, they could still be met (at least in theory) from the group of young men and women with I.Q.'s of 113 and over. Having regard to the forseeable needs of the future and to the possible range of what could still justly be described as higher education, it is far more this target of 18 or 20 per cent, rather than the recently proposed 10 per cent or the present 4 or 5 per cent, which I should regard as both desirable and justifiable.[1]

I very much doubt whether an increase of this order could be attained simply by manipulating the selection procedures now used in primary or secondary education, and I am con-

---

[1] This was written before the publication of the Robbins' Committee Report and without knowledge of the recommendations of that Committee. But I am convinced that a proportion of around twenty per cent should be our target for expansion over the next generation. There will no doubt be University voices raised against this. But in part this will be because of our tradition that the universities should concentrate on honours courses of a relatively specialised kind. My own view is that we need a considerable expansion of general degrees at the undergraduate level and, at the same time, a corresponding increase in much more specialised graduate study. At the same time it is undoubtedly true that the rate of expansion of higher education will depend heavily upon what can be done to increase the effectiveness of primary and secondary education.

vinced that we should not use them for such a purpose.[1] For in any case, those procedures are not efficient. There is no sharp and unmistakable cut-off point at the break between primary and secondary education, between the children who would and those who would not be likely to profit from an 'academic' type of curriculum. Nor is it inevitable that the purely 'academic' curriculum should be the only preparation for higher education; that depends upon the scope and content of higher education. Our selection procedures at the point of transfer between secondary and higher education are also imperfect.[2] It would in many respects be preferable to admit considerably larger proportions of boys and girls to the universities and to allow them to try their capacities against whatever may be the 'normal' examinations used to test performance in specific subjects. Self-selection of this kind would be more just than pre-selection. And if it meant that, as in some state universities in the U.S.A., large numbers of students did not go beyond one year of college studies, this is not necessarily harmful. On the contrary, I believe that there is much to be said for guaranteeing the right of entry to one year of higher education to all who attain reasonable levels of competence in their secondary schools.[3] Modifying and post-

[1] Nor would the abandonment of the present 'objective' selection tests help if the secondary school system remains unchanged. On the contrary, the replacement of such tests by, for example, teachers' reports might simply result in a less justifiable selection of children for the different types of secondary education. 'Objective' tests would be very valuable if used for purposes of guidance rather than for early selection. For a balanced and most informed discussion of the use of tests in this way, see National Foundation for Educational Research, *Procedures for the allocation of pupils in secondary education*, London, 1963.

[2] In any case, university teachers are often ambivalent about what constitutes 'capacity to profit from a university education'. They tend to worry when the proportion of first-class honours falls; but many (and not infrequently those who worry about 'firsts') would reject the idea of developing tests which might select only those students most likely to achieve 'firsts' and 'upper seconds'. And this ambivalence is understandable, for the purpose of a university is not solely to produce 'firsts' and 'upper seconds'.

[3] But not beyond one year unless sufficient competence is shown. And not necessarily guaranteeing the right to financial support. I do not regard the abolition of means tests for university maintenance grants as justifiable—or, at least, not unless there is an obligation on the part of students to undertake

poning selection in this way would make it possible to offer to a much larger fraction of the new generations the kind of education which should help them to face an inevitably more complex technology and to meet with greater competence the responsibilities of citizenship. Of course the cost would be great. But if we are an affluent society, what better use could be made of part of our affluence—as well as of part of our extended expectation of life—than in supplying the foundations for a more instructed citizenship.

Educational change on the scale implied will, however, require to go far beyond removing the constraints imposed by the undue application of selection tests at too early an age and by the segregation of children into educationally privileged and underprivileged groups. The nature and potentialities of different forms of educational institutions at the various levels will need to be re-examined and the experiments now taking place in a number of areas will require to be extended and their results assessed. The contents of the curriculum will demand scrutiny, and especially the practicable range of courses in higher education. Above all, educational change will have to concern itself positively with efforts to involve children and young people in the processes of learning and discovery. Dr Douglas rightly emphasises that much more research will be needed here, and not least into the means of intensifying the intellectual stimulus of the environment in the pre-school and early school years. But we now know sufficient—and Dr Douglas himself has contributed greatly to our knowledge—to see where some of the new research should direct itself and also to initiate experiments both in teaching as such and in attempts to secure a more effective collaboration between the teacher, the parent and the child. And we can envisage the kinds of change in the

---

a period of national service after graduation, including in the term national service such employment as teaching, hospital service, and various forms of public service (at home or overseas). If it is objected, in respect of teaching, that there would be both reluctance and excessive turnover, I can only plead that both these conditions apply to some extent now and could scarcely be made worse by employing new graduates as temporary teaching assistants.

responsibilities and status of teachers at the primary and
secondary levels which might facilitate that more effective
collaboration.[1] How much can be done and how quickly will
depend upon many factors, though postponement will not
make the process any easier, for the numbers of children and
young people are growing.[2] But even if progress is necessarily
slower than would be hoped, the minimum required—and
that as soon as possible—is a comprehensive development
programme, endorsed by parliament and so presented as to
leave no doubt that its implementation will begin by a
specified date.

September 1963

[1] I cannot refrain from citing a letter written by John Dury (a follower
of Comenius) in 1642, on the problems of education. 'The meanes then to
advance humane learning, and the reformation of schools is to elaborate
certain treaties and to put them that they may be made use of by all. The
first of these treaties should be a discovery of the defects and of the disorders
in teaching and educating children, with the intimation of the remedies
thereof, and of the manner of applying the same unto the disease, which
should be done briefly and substantially. The second should be a direction
for parents, how to implant into their children the seeds of vertue and to
beget in them a disposition towards learning'. (R. F. Young, *Comenius in
England*, London 1932, pp. 72–73.) Perhaps we shall soon know enough to
being to write the treatises which Dury had in mind.

[2] I am indebted to my research assistant, Dr S. Thapar, for the following
data on children and young persons in Great Britain, derived from the
official population projections of the Registrars General:

No. of persons (thousands)

Age (years)	Date:		
	1963	1970	1980
5–10	4579	5401	5852
11–14	3123	3194	3826
15–17	2576	2247	2764
18–20	2218	2236	2627

CHAPTER I

The Scope of this Book

IN RECENT years the efficiency of our educational system has become a subject of intense concern to many people, both in academic circles and outside them. At a time when individual competitiveness is being transferred progressively from the economic to the educational world and from the office or workshop to the school and university,[1] and when international rivalry is increasing in the technical field, it is vital that we should offer all children the opportunity to develop their abilities and aptitudes to the full.

There is widespread belief that since the Education Act of 1944 the social waste, which in the 1920s occurred at the time when children were selected for secondary schools, has been 'pushed forward *into* the grammar schools where it now occurs at the threshold of the Sixth Form'.[2]

Today, the primary schools are seen by many as offering uniform educational opportunity, and the 11 + secondary selection examination is widely accepted as 'probably the most efficient examination in the educational system and more valid than those for entering the civil service, universities or various professions'.[3] There is, of course, a unique quality about the secondary selection examination which makes such comparisons invalid. A child who wishes to enter a university, for example, has many to apply to and may try for a place in successive years, whereas a child who sits the 11 + examination must accept the result or move into the private educational system.

An examination of the opportunities provided by a few selected local authorities has led to a belief that the existing waste in education largely occurs through early leaving from the grammar schools. This belief takes no account of the many differences in educational opportunities and in the methods of secondary school

[1] Marshall, T. H. (1950).
[2] Flood, J. E. *et al.* (1957).
[3] Yates, A., and Pidgeon, D. A. (1958).

selection that exist between one local education authority and another. For example, there are great variations in the distribution of grammar school places in different parts of the country, and it has yet to be shown that they conform to the geographical distribution of measured ability in children. Within a single local education authority, moreover, the severity of competition for grammar school entry may change as new industries develop; the opening of a new factory or government department may alter the social structure of an area so much that competition for a limited number of grammar school places becomes more intense and children are excluded who, in previous years, would have been given places. Then there are considerable local differences in the methods used for selecting children for secondary schools: the importance placed on measured ability, teachers' reports and examination papers varies greatly between different areas and sometimes, over the years, within the same area. There is evidence that these variations may affect the opportunities open to children from different social classes, for when standardised mental and performance tests are dropped, as has been the recent practice in several areas, the chances of grammar school entry for manual working class children decline.[1]

These and similar considerations lead one to suspect that there are still both social and regional inequalities leading to waste at the time when children are being selected for secondary schools. And still further back, children who have to face apathy at home, poor teaching at school and the contempt of their class mates for the process of learning, are unlikely to succeed in their studies or to stand as good a chance in the 11+ examination as children of comparable ability, who have not had to contend with adverse circumstances such as these. It may be thought that this is a type of inequality which can be removed only by profound social changes that may take a generation or more to achieve. This is not necessarily a true conclusion. Perhaps deficiencies in the home or community can be offset, and social inequalities of opportunity reduced, by raising the standard of teaching in the primary schools or by altering the methods of streaming by ability.

In recent years there has been much discussion about the size

[1] Floud, J. E., and Halsey, A. H. (1957).

of the 'pool of ability', a term which is used to describe those persons in the population who are capable of benefiting academically from a university education. They are often defined as the ones who show this level of ability at eighteen years, a definition that ignores the question of how much ability has seeped away from the pool at earlier ages. It is important, from many points of view, to know how large the pool would be if there were no leakage of talent, but till now there has been no means of making an informed guess at its size. To do so, we would require information on the educational progress of a group of children followed from early life through their school careers; a group, moreover, containing children from every type of home and every part of the country; in other words a true national sample. In this way the dimensions of educational wastage would be established; and if, in addition, the educational achievement of these children could be seen against the background of their homes and schools, we would learn what sort of children were being lost and the reasons for losing them.

The National Survey of Health and Development provides just such a sample, and during the sixteen years it has been in progress, a unique body of social and educational information has been collected about 5,362 children living in England, Wales and Scotland. In this book, we follow the children who were enrolled in this survey through their years in the primary schools until they have sat the secondary selection examinations at 11+ and are allocated to their secondary schools. Subsequent reports will review the progress of these same children in their secondary schools, technical colleges and universities; so that a complete picture will in time be obtained of the educational opportunities enjoyed by a national sample of children, and of the way in which these opportunities have been influenced by the homes and schools. The history of this inquiry and the information that it provides are described in the next chapter.

CHAPTER II

Sources of Information

THE CHILDREN in this survey[1] are drawn from every type of family and every part of the country. Their parents include at one extreme eminent artists, scientists and politicians and, at the other, unemployed labourers. They are scattered all over Great Britain from the Scilly Isles to the Shetlands. For the purpose of this study, however, the children at school in Scotland are excluded, on the ground that they are selected for secondary education at a different age and in a different manner from those at English or Welsh schools. Early leaving among the Scottish children is briefly discussed in the last chapter; on this aspect legitimate comparisons may be made between Scotland and the rest of Great Britain.

All the children have one thing in common: they were born during the first week of March 1946. Illegitimate children and twins were excluded, but apart from this all children born during this week to the wives of non-manual workers and of farm labourers, and one-quarter of those born to the wives of other types of manual workers and self-employed persons are included. This method of social selection reduces to manageable proportions the number of children to be kept under observation; at the same time it enriches the sample with middle-class and agricultural workers' children whose attitudes and opportunities for education are of special interest. For these groups the survey gives as much information as would be obtained from a sample more than twice its size. When required, the social structure of the original national population of children can be regained by inflating the number of manual workers' and self-employed workers' children four times. When this is done estimates of mortality, fertility, grammar school allocation, etc., are reached which correspond closely with those from national sources. These

[1] A full description of the survey is given in *Maternity in Great Britain*, Oxford University Press (1948), and in *Children under Five*, by J. W. B. Douglas and J. M. Blomfield, Allen & Unwin (1958).

4

are referred to as 'population estimates' and all figures are of this type unless otherwise stated.

The greater part of the educational information used in this study was provided by the primary and preparatory school teachers, who kept special records of school absences and the reasons for them, and reported at intervals on the behaviour of the children at school and on their attitudes to work. They also supervised the giving of a series of tests of mental ability and school achievement, when the children were eight years old and again, when they were eleven, a few weeks before they took the secondary selection examinations. Lastly, the teachers assessed the level of interest the parents showed in their children's school progress and gave an account of the parents' visits to the primary schools. The headmasters described the location and amenities of the schools, the type of children who came as pupils, and their past successes in the secondary selection examinations.

Information about the health of the children was provided by the school doctors, who gave them special clinical examinations on three occasions, the last at eleven years just before they took the selection examinations. On each occasion medical histories were given by the parents, after which the children were weighed and measured and given a detailed physical examination which included tests of visual acuity and, at eleven years, an assessment of physical maturity.

Additional information on the health of the children was given by the health visitors and school nurses who visited their homes on the average once a year. They recorded all accidents, hospital admissions and out-patient or clinic attendances, and asked the mothers about all absences from school of more than a week's duration. They were also the chief source of information about the children's families and home circumstances and they have provided, at intervals from eight years onwards, information about the educational aspirations of the parents for their children and the jobs they wish them to take on leaving school.

The last source of information was the local education authorities who, in addition to organising the questionnaire surveys and arranging for the tests to be given, informed us in June 1958 of the results of the secondary selection examinations.

By using these different sources of information we see the

same children through many eyes and can compare the opinions of mothers and teachers with the scores made in achievement tests completed by the children themselves, and with the results of the 11 + selection examinations. The reliability of the information may be checked by comparing the answers given in one year with those given in the next, and by comparing one source of information with another; by seeing, for example, the amount of agreement or disagreement there is between the teachers and mothers when they are asked the same questions. In these ways we avoid many of the disadvantages encountered when information is provided by numerous and widely scattered agents who cannot be individually briefed or supervised.

The help given by teachers, doctors and health visitors allowed many events in these children's lives to be recorded as they occurred and others while they were still fresh in their mothers' memories. In this way many of the distortions and re-interpretations were avoided that are apt to occur when one looks back and tries to fit remembered events into a pattern of causation. Parents with difficult children, for example, tend to seek an explanation for their bad behaviour and often find it in a popular psychological theory. If they have read about the effects of maternal deprivation on the emotional development of children, they may well rummage out of their memories a history of early separation which would never have been recalled if the child were not a cause for anxiety. In this study, however, for all children, both normal and abnormal, we have uniform historical records which can be related to their later development without danger of being warped by preconceived ideas or lapses of memory.

Some further comment is needed on the mental ability and school performance tests which were devised for this inquiry by the National Foundation for Educational Research in England and Wales.[1] These were group tests, but were given to individual survey children who were supervised by their teachers when they filled them in. When the children were eight years and three months old they completed four tests, one of picture intelligence and the others of sentence completion, reading and vocabulary. Just before their eleventh birthday, and a few weeks before they took the secondary selection examinations, a second group of tests

[1] Details are given in Appendix I, page 129.

was given. The reading and vocabulary tests which had been given at eight years were repeated in exactly the same form, a new intelligence test was given, and an arithmetic one was substituted for the sentence completion which had been given at eight. Whereas the problems in the eight-year intelligence test were presented in picture form, half of those in the eleven-year test were presented as diagrams and the remainder in words. Two separate scores accordingly are available for the eleven-year intelligence test; one is called the 'non-verbal' score, and the other the 'verbal'. The scores made by children in all these tests were converted, as is usual in this type of study, into T scores which were designed so that the average score for all children in the population (see page 5) is 50 and the standard deviation 10; for example, a child who has a score of 60 lies one standard deviation above the average score made by all children in that test: he is, in other words, in the top 16 per cent of the group.

The T scores place children in order according to their success or failure in answering the questions set in each test. At each age and in each test the children are being compared with each other, and the scores they achieve do not show the absolute degree of excellence or incompetence of their performance nor, when comparing one age with another, do they show the extent to which there has been an absolute change in performance. For a study such as this, interest centres on the way in which some children pull ahead and others lag behind in their school work and in their ability to solve test problems. The T scores used here provide the most satisfactory way of describing relative changes of this type.

Some readers may be better acquainted with intelligence quotients (I.Q.s) than with T scores. They are equivalent measures, except that the I.Q. has a mean of 100 and a standard deviation of 15[1] and the T scores have a mean of 50 and a standard deviation of 10. The reliability and validity of the tests is discussed on page 130 by D. A. Pidgeon, Senior Research Officer of the National Foundation for Educational Research in England and Wales.

It was necessary to decide whether to treat the test scores individually or to combine them to give an average score at each

---

[1] To convert T scores into I.Q.s the following formula may be used

$$\text{I.Q.} = 25 + 1\cdot5 \text{ (T score)}$$

age. At first sight it would seem logical to separate the mental ability (or intelligence) scores from the school achievement scores, as a poor school or home environment might be expected to exert a more depressing influence on the latter. Moreover, a comparison of the scores made on these two types of test might reveal a group of children who were 'under-achievers' in the sense that their school performance lagged behind their measured intelligence. Some other children, of course, would do better in the school performance tests than their measured intelligence would justify (i.e. 'over-achievers'), and it seemed that these two groups of children, if they could be isolated, might give a clue to the way in which educational progress is influenced by the quality of the homes and schools. It was soon evident, however, that a comparison of these two types of test was not profitable. With a few exceptions, the circumstances which are associated with a deterioration in the scores for the school achievement tests are equally associated with a deterioration in the mental ability scores, and so there seemed to be no point in making a distinction between the two types of test used in this study. The educational analysis has accordingly been simplified by taking at each age the average of the four tests. As these tests are highly inter-correlated[1] the resultant average scores have also a mean of approximately 50. The standard deviations of these average test scores are 8·4 at eight years and 8·9 at eleven.

While the potential value of longitudinal studies of education is widely acknowledged, they are in disfavour as being costly, difficult to analyse and subject to heavy loss and unpredictable distortion. They are also unattractive to some because of the length of time that must elapse before results are available. These views are based on the experience of studies, mostly in America, in which large volumes of information were collected about small numbers of children living in single towns or limited geographical areas. These types of study absorb the energies of many highly trained staff, and since many families move out of the area of study they are wasteful of effort. Moreover, those that move out tend to differ from those that stay put, so there is a progressive change in the characteristics of the families under study, making it difficult to interpret the results.

[1] See Appendix I, pages 130 and 132.

In the present survey costs have been kept low by the generous help given by the education and public health departments of local authorities. Losses have also been small because the whole country was our parish and children could be lost only if they died or went abroad, if they were untraced, or if their parents refused to give information. The important question now is whether these losses have biased the sample to such an extent that it no longer gives a true picture of those who took their 11 + selection examinations in 1957.

The balance sheet of the survey is shown in Table IIa (page 141). By March 1957, 4·9 per cent of the children had died and 6·7 per cent had emigrated with their families. As a source of bias these losses may be discounted since they represent a natural decrease in the survey population which can hardly be regarded as distorting the sample, even though the children who died tended to come from the manual working classes, and those who emigrated from the middle classes. The high death-rate in the manual working classes fell particularly heavily on the boys; in this survey 161 of them died for every 100 girls, whereas in the middle classes only 113 died for every 100 girls. As a result, by the time they were eleven, there were proportionately more boys in the middle than in the manual working classes, although at birth the proportion of boys in each of these classes was similar.

No arrangements were made to enrol children who since 1946 have entered this country from abroad, the West Indies for example, and for this reason the sample has become progressively very slightly less representative of the whole national population of school children born in 1946. But even if it had been possible to enrol these immigrants, little would have been gained, since early information on their upbringing and abilities would have been lacking—information which forms the basis of this study.

Details of secondary school allocation are known for 97 per cent of the 4,195 survey children still remaining in England and Wales, and it is probable that some of the absent 3 per cent have left the country. That the remaining children may, in fact, be taken as a representative group of all those of the same age at school in England and Wales, is shown by comparing their secondary school allocation with the figures published by the Ministry of Education. There is close agreement between the proportions of children at different types of school shown by the Ministry and by the survey. Private school children appear to be slightly under-represented in the survey and grammar school children slightly over-represented but these are small and compensatory differences; the total proportion of children in selective secondary schools of all types is 27 per cent both in the survey sample and in the Ministry's figures.[1]

The main purpose of this report is to describe the test performance of children coming from different home backgrounds and to relate these to the results of the secondary selection examinations. Children failed to take the tests for a variety of reasons: a few could not be traced, some were absent from school, a few were too backward to be tested, some had parents who refused to allow them to sit the tests and a few were at schools which could not set aside the time for testing or arrange the necessary supervision. For these reasons only 81·5 per cent of the survey children who were at school in England and Wales in 1957 had taken tests at both eight and eleven years, and it is only these who are included in this study. It is important to know what sort of children were not tested, so that some estimate may be made of the extent to which the structure of the survey sample has been distorted by their loss.

A rather high proportion of the children who were not tested at eight or eleven were at private schools, particularly at small ones, and owing to this, there is a social bias in the losses since many of the children who are excluded come from middle class families. Even so this distortion is small. Of the 3,418 children who sat both series of tests 569 were the sons or daughters of professional or salaried workers, whereas if there had been no selective loss 628 would have come from these types of family. There are also fewer boys than would have been expected if the losses had been random. These largely come from manual working class families where instead of the 902 boys for whom we have full records one might expect there would be 920. The social class bias is the only considerable distortion found. For all other characteristics of the sample (apart from test scores) that could be examined, the exclusion of these children led to changes which

[1] See Table II(b), page 142. Selective secondary schools are Grammar, Independent, and Technical.

are no more than those which might occur by chance if the sample were replaced by another of the same size and age.

When assessing social class differences in secondary selection, interest centres on those children who are competing for grammar school places in the 11 + examinations. These include some of the children at private schools, though many at these schools are excluded. The criterion for inclusion in this part of the analysis is that a secondary selection examination should have been taken or, failing this, that the children proceeded at 11 + to local education authority secondary schools or grant-aided schools, which could be distinguished as grammar, technical or secondary modern.[1] There were 3,809 children who met these requirements, and of these 3,297 had completed the survey tests at both eight and eleven years. The losses here (13 per cent) are smaller than those described in the last paragraph but one and they are also less socially biased; there are, for example, 510 children whose fathers were salaried workers or in the professions as compared with an expected 530 children if there had been an equal loss from all social classes. In this and, as far as can be ascertained, in all other respects the loss of untested children from the group used for the study of secondary selection in the various social classes has led to a negligible distortion of the characteristics of the parent sample.

The average test scores of the children examined in this educational analysis are 50·23 in the eight-year tests and 50·25 in the eleven-year tests; these figures are a little above the average for all children tested at these ages (50·06 and 50·13 are the average scores made by the whole population of children at eight and eleven years respectively). It seems that although there has been a heavier loss of private school children, it has been the duller ones that failed to take the tests on both occasions (the average score for children tested at eight but missing at eleven is 47·96, and the average for those tested at eleven but not at eight is 46·92).

There is another possible source of bias to consider. By keeping these children under observation, by testing them and discussing

[1] Children who were placed in grammar, technical or secondary modern streams of comprehensive or multilateral schools are included in the appropriate type of selective secondary school.

their school progress with their mothers, we may have altered their attitude to their work, and increased the interest taken by their parents in their school careers. To test this we traced one-third of the manual workers' children who, though born in the survey week, had been excluded from the national survey study (see page 4) and compared their 11+ results with those of an equivalent group of survey children. As they had been neither tested nor visited in their homes the former group might have been expected to be less successful in the 11+ examination, but this was not so; 15·6 per cent of them went to grammar schools as compared with 15·0 per cent of the equivalent group of survey children.[1]

The general conclusion, then, is that this sample of children can be safely used to describe the experience of all those children in England and Wales who were of an age to take the 11+ selection examinations in March 1957. Small biases do exist but can have only a trivial effect.

Since the beginning of this study a great deal of information has been amassed about the children, their parents, homes and schools. As this was collected, it was punched on Hollerith cards and stored, and from this store new cards can be rapidly built up to cover any special field of interest; this report, for example, is largely based on tables derived from a single card which describes the educational progress of the children and bears information culled from some sixty earlier cards. Because of the nature of this particular study much detailed information had to be simplified and summarised to bring it to a manageable size. The types of home the children were living in, for example, are described in four simplified codes which summarise ownership, crowding, sleeping arrangements, amenities, and the changes of these over the years. And for the final analysis these codes have been further combined. This process of summarisation has been largely done by rule of thumb, that is to say by sorting and re-sorting the cards until groups were reached which were both large enough for statistical analysis and showed the maximum differences in average test performance and 11+ examination results. More sophisticated methods might have produced rather more effective

[1] These children are of course drawn solely from the manual working classes and the self-employed—hence the low proportion going to grammar schools.

groupings of some of the information, but the application of these to the estimation of standards of child care and levels of school interest suggested that any advantage from this approach was likely to be marginal.

In presenting the results of this study I have put the majority of tables in Appendix III, so that the flow of the text is not constantly interrupted, while the statistically curious reader can see the evidence on which the major conclusions are based. The text describes the conclusions reached after examining many hundreds of tables, only a few of which can be published owing to the limits of space. Some of the conclusions which are lightly touched on here will be the subject of more intensive description in subsequent publications.

I have seldom calculated simple tests of statistical significance, as they are likely to be misleading when used to give authority to conclusions reached in a study such as this. To show, for example, that there is a statistically significant difference in the average intelligence test scores of early and late maturing girls, means nothing until other factors of home and family background have been taken into account. My aim has been to establish the presence of consistent trends of performance, and then, having decided which factors are outstanding, to use relatively sophisticated statistical methods to try to unravel their overlapping effects and to show the ways in which they vary in importance as the children grow older. This approach was made possible by the advice and help of H. R. Simpson of Rothamsted Experimental Station, and his description of the statistical method used and its results will be found in Appendix II (page 133).

CHAPTER III

Selecting Children for Secondary School

By 1938 it was widely realised that 'the existing arrangements for the whole-time higher education of boys and girls above the age of eleven in England and Wales [had] ceased to correspond with the actual structure of modern society and with the economic facts of the situation'.[1] At that time more than half the gifted children did not get beyond the elementary school, and one child in five was given a standard of education for which he was unsuited; a standard more often too low than too high.[2]

The expressed aim of the 1944 Education Act was to remedy this situation and to provide all children with the type of secondary education best matched to their abilities. A primary, or preparatory school system should be available for all children up to the age of 11+, followed by varying forms of secondary education corresponding to their different talents and capacities after that age.

It was not originally intended that selection for secondary schools should be by competitive examination. Indeed it was felt that 'there is nothing to be said in favour of a system which subjects children at the age of eleven to the strain of a competitive examination on which, not only their future schooling, but their future careers may depend'.[3] Such a system would be likely to have undesirable effects on the primary school curriculum as well as on the children. It was hoped that in the future 'children at the age of eleven should be classified . . . on an assessment of their individual aptitudes by such means as school records supplemented if necessary by intelligence tests, due regard being had to their parents' wishes and the careers they have in mind'. This classification should be subject to review as the children's

[1] Spens, W. (1938).
[2] Hogben, L. (1938).
[3] Board of Education (1943).

14

special gifts and capacities develop and the free interchange of pupils from one type of secondary education to another should be made easy. It was clear that no method of selection would work satisfactorily unless enough grammar school places were provided to permit a grammar school education for those children who, all things considered, would benefit more from such a course than from any other form of secondary education.

The present methods of selecting children for secondary schools vary greatly from one local education authority area to another. Few are of the non-competitive type envisaged at the time of the 1944 Act, and most authorities use combinations of mental tests, teachers' reports, written examinations and interviews. Some require all children to sit the selection examinations, others only those who reach a certain level in preliminary tests; but even this in many cases is not a rigid rule and any child may proceed to the main examination if his parents so wish.

The type of child going to grammar school is to some extent determined by the methods used in secondary selection. In Middlesbrough and South-West Hertfordshire, for example, virtually all boys with the necessary minimum measured intelligence from each occupational group were awarded grammar school places when selection was made by a combination of tests, examinations, teachers' reports and interviews. But when tests were abandoned in South-West Hertfordshire the proportion of working class boys gaining grammar school places fell and that of middle class boys rose. This probably reflected the social biases of subjective judgements at interview and of the teachers' assessments.[1]

Career prospects increasingly depend on academic success in early life and the award of a grammar school place has come to be taken by many as a badge of success for primary school children. This would not be so if it were generally accepted by the parents that each child was being given the type of education best suited to his abilities; but in a situation where grammar school places are limited in number and awarded on the results of a competitive examination, it is not surprising that parents should take another view.

[1] Floud, J. E., and Halsey, A. H. (1957). A similar conclusion is reached by Yates, A., and Pidgeon, D. A. (1957).

If there is secondary selection at the age of eleven there should also be opportunities at later ages for the free exchange of pupils between one type of secondary school and another, so that faulty selection may be remedied and the later-developing child be given the type of education which makes full use of his ability. This is not easy to achieve. Few Directors of Education are willing to offend the *amour propre* of parents by transferring their children from grammar schools to those of another type, for though it was originally intended that there should be parity of esteem between the three types of secondary school, in practice the grammar school has the highest status. There are also difficulties in transferring children from secondary modern schools to grammar schools, since subjects such as French or Algebra may have been taught in the former at only a low level if at all.

After these preliminary observations we will look at the details of secondary selection in 1957 as recorded in this survey. Scottish children, as already mentioned, are excluded from the following discussion, and when the results of secondary selection are described, children at private schools who did not compete in the 11+ examinations, are excluded. There is a further reason for excluding them: many transfers to private schools take place when the children are twelve or thirteen, which is outside the age range of this book. It is evident, however, that by leaving the private system of education out of account we are ignoring an important source of secondary schooling which is largely used by the upper social classes; a source, moreover, that makes an increasingly important contribution to the stream of secondary education as the children grow older, since these schools more than others tend to retain their pupils after the age of fifteen. For these reasons some observations on the opportunities provided by private education are made in the last chapter (see page 122), using the information which has recently been collected on later transfers to private schools. Observations will also be found in this chapter on the contribution made by technical schools to the secondary education of children from different social classes. Here again a considerable number of children transfer to these schools at twelve or thirteen so that the position at eleven under-estimates the importance of this type of education.

In England and Wales, according to the present survey, 19·1 per cent of all children go to grammar schools. This figure includes among the grammar school children those who are in the grammar streams of comprehensive or multilateral schools and those in grant-aided grammar schools. It agrees well with the figure of 18·3 per cent given by the Ministry of Education for the proportion of thirteen-year-old children in grammar schools in 1959.[1] In some ways, however, it is an unrealistic figure, for children in private schools or in comprehensive schools with no clearly defined grammar and non-grammar streams are treated as if they were competing for grammar school places but failing to get them. A more satisfactory figure, for the purpose of this report, is obtained when the number of children at grammar schools or in grammar streams is related to the total number who competed for places. It then appears that 20·9 per cent of the children who compete for grammar school places get them. How far does this allocation of places satisfy the parents' wishes, and meet the teachers' views on the proportion of children that could profit from a grammar school education?

By the time the children are eight years old, 49 per cent of their mothers have chosen their secondary school by name and a further 38 per cent by type. In the intervening years they maintain their early preferences, though a few (12 per cent) of those who hoped for a grammar school place appear to take a more realistic view of their children's abilities as the secondary selection examinations approach and adjust their choice from a grammar to a secondary modern school.[2]

More than half the mothers wish their children to go to grammar schools rather than to secondary modern schools, and cultural or political opposition to the former type of school hardly shows itself. Sixty-two per cent when their children were eight years old hoped they would gain a grammar school place. Only 2·3 per cent of parents said they would refuse a place if it were offered their child, the most common reasons being lack of the necessary ability, preference for a private school, or distance from the nearest grammar school. None of these children

[1] Table II(b), page 142.
[2] At eleven, just before the selection examinations 97% had chosen the type of secondary school they wished their children to go to.

did in fact go to a grammar school. Very few mothers objected to grammar schools on 'social' grounds and these were often ambiguous—such statements as 'no other person in the family has been there' or 'children ought to leave school at fifteen' are open to a variety of interpretations. No mother based her objections on the possibility that her child might absorb different ideas and social values and grow away from the family. Other opinions might have been voiced by the fathers if they, rather than the mothers, had answered these questions.

Only 2 per cent of the children whose parents wished them to go to secondary modern schools and leave at sixteen or earlier were offered grammar school places, and all accepted them. Their later progress at school will be observed with interest; will they leave earlier than the other grammar school pupils, and will their parents' aspirations rise now that their children have the chance of higher education?

There is no doubt of the high status accorded to the grammar type of education, but its aims seem to be frequently misunderstood. Nearly half the mothers who want their children to go to grammar schools intend to take them away when they are sixteen or younger, and so appear to wish for this type of education for non-academic reasons. Thirty-one per cent of all mothers want their children to stay on at grammar schools until they are seventeen or older, and I have taken this as the minimum estimate of the real demand for grammar school places. It is by no means fully met, and 59 per cent are disappointed in their hopes.

A few mothers were so antagonistic to secondary modern schools that they said they would send their children to private schools if they were not given grammar school places, but few of those who said this actually did so when the occasion arose. Only 5 per cent of all the children who were not given the grammar school place their parents wished for were removed to private schools,[1] and this figure undoubtedly exaggerates the protest, for 2 per cent of the children who were accepted by grammar schools and whose mothers had no reason to be discontented, were sent to private schools instead.

That the results of the secondary selection examinations are

[1] This was the position in June 1958 when the children were twelve years old.

accepted does not mean that the parents are satisfied either with the number of places available or with the fairness of the selection methods—indeed many letters received by us express bitter resentment. But unless there is a private school nearby and the money to pay its fees, there is little they can do. We know that some parents asked the Directors of Education to reconsider their children's 11+ allocation, but with the limited number of grammar school places available few alterations were possible and the number of children originally given a secondary modern school place who were later transferred to grammar schools was only sufficient to fill the vacancies created in the latter by the transfer of children from grammar to private schools.

A relatively large proportion of grammar school children (34 per cent) will leave school, so their mothers say, at sixteen or earlier, but now they have established themselves at these schools perhaps their parents may change their views. In contrast, the mothers of 13 per cent of the children at secondary modern schools hope they will stay at school till they are seventeen or older—or did so before they took the selection examinations. Seventy-nine per cent of these children were expected to get grammar rather than secondary modern school places, and it may now be that their parents' aspirations will change. Further, the children themselves may yield to the pressures for early leaving which, so often, are strongly present in secondary modern schools.

The primary school teachers would like 29 per cent of their pupils to go to grammar schools. This is similar to the mothers' wishes, but of course the teachers do not always choose the same children; only 56 per cent of the children they would like to send to grammar schools have mothers who wish them to go and are prepared to keep them there until seventeen. We shall see later that the teachers' views are governed by other considerations than the ability of the children. But in most areas they play a part in deciding the results of the selection examinations, and it is not unexpected that 64 per cent of the children considered suitable for grammar school by their teachers actually went there, and that, out of all the children given places, only 13 per cent would have been excluded if their teachers' recommendations had been followed.

Before proceeding further, it is necessary to look at the test scores of the children in relation to their performance in the 11+ examinations. For many reasons a perfect agreement is not to be expected; any test or examination is only an estimate of ability and subject to error; moreover, 11+ selection is generally based not only on test scores but also on teachers' assessments, on written papers and sometimes on interviews. There is, however, a practical value in seeing what proportion of able children, judging ability by the survey tests, fail to get grammar school places and conversely what proportion of relatively less able children get them. It is of immediate value in helping us to understand the influence of the home and the school on educational selection and of more remote value when at a later stage we can look back at the secondary school careers of these children and try to assess how far ability has been wasted and for what reasons.

It will be remembered (see page 6) that special tests of mental ability and school achievement were given to the survey children a few weeks before they sat the secondary selection examinations. There is, as one would expect, a large measure of agreement between the results of these tests and the results of the examinations. While the only children who are certain of going to grammar schools are those who score 70 or over in the tests, few of those who score between 61 and 69 fail to get places. At the other end of the scale of ability, grammar school places are seldom given to children who score less than 55.

	Level of Test Score at Eleven							
	48 *or less*	49–51	52–54	55–57	58–60	61–63	64–66	67 *and over*
	%	%	%	%	%	%	%	%
Award of grammar school places	0·2	2·7	9·2	27·2	47·9	83·8	85·5	91·9

The following table shows the distribution of the test scores of eleven-year-old children according to the type of secondary school they were attending in 1957. It underlines the extent to which children in local education authority schools are segregated by ability as measured in our tests. In contrast, those at private schools are drawn from a much wider range of measured ability— they include clever children as well as some relatively backward ones and the average test score of the children going to them is much below the average for those at grammar schools, but considerably above the average for those at secondary modern schools.

	Grammar School Children	Technical School Children	Independent School Children	Secondary Modern School Children
Average test score at eleven years	60·98	56·60	53·18	47·05
Range within which 90 per cent of T scores fall in each type of school	54–68	50–65	40–66	34–59

The mother's aspirations appear to have an influence on the allocation of her child, particularly if his measured ability is such that he is likely in any case to have some difficulty in getting a grammar school place. For example, among children scoring between 55 and 57 in the eleven-year tests, as many as 42 per cent reach the grammar schools if their mothers definitely wish them to go there, 21 per cent if they are undecided and only 8 per cent if they originally chose a secondary modern school.[1] Similar differences, though less marked, are found at higher levels of test score and the picture is consistent throughout. After taking account of the distribution of measured ability in the three groups of children (and also of their social class and the geographical area in which they live) the position may be summarised by saying that those whose mothers want them to go to grammar school and stay there until they are seventeen get 11 per cent more grammar school places than expected, those whose mothers

[1] Table III(a), page 143.

are undecided get 8 per cent fewer places than expected, and those whose mothers want them to go to secondary modern schools and leave early get 60 per cent fewer places than expected. In other words it seems that children who are encouraged by their parents do better in the selection examinations than their measured ability would predict and those who are not encouraged do worse.

The teachers' assessments of the ability of children to benefit from a grammar school education agree with these figures in suggesting that there is a particularly high wastage in the selection examinations among those who are expected by their parents to go to secondary modern schools. These children get less than half the grammar school places they deserve according to their teachers, who see a much greater wastage among them than among those whose parents are more ambitious for their educational success.

The conclusions of this chapter may be summarised as follows. While no mother objects to secondary selection on political or social grounds, many are unsatisfied with the results of selection, which meet only two-thirds of their demands for grammar school places. The teachers, too, feel that places are available for only two-thirds of the children who would benefit from them.

A third of the children who actually go to grammar schools have mothers who intend to take them away from school when they are sixteen or younger. Since this intention was expressed before their children had sat the 11+ examinations, however, they may now change their minds. The mothers' attitudes have an important influence on the chances of their children getting grammar school places, particularly if their measured ability is at a level where grammar school entry is in the balance.

CHAPTER IV

Regional Inequalities in Selection

IT WAS emphasised in the Spens report on secondary education published in 1938 that 'no method of choice can work satisfactorily unless there are enough grammar school places to secure a grammar school education for those children who, all things considered, will benefit more from such a course than from other forms of secondary education'. We have seen in the previous chapter that both mothers and teachers feel that the places provided fall short of the needs of the children. But even accepting for the moment the fact that in the whole country only 19 per cent of children can follow grammar school courses, it is essential, if we are to make proper use of these places, that they should be distributed throughout the country according to the known ability of children. This, as we now show, does not appear to be the case.

The proportion of children going to grammar schools varies from one local education authority to another: in some authorities places are given to more than 30 per cent of children, in others to less than 10 per cent.[1] These differences, as the Ministry of Education points out, do not necessarily imply unequal opportunities for secondary education. When, as in some areas, there are many private schools, the demand for grammar school places may be low. Moreover the academic ability of children may vary in different parts of the country and so may their parents' views on the value of a grammar school education. We may also, when making the broad classification of schools into 'grammar' and 'other', fail to do justice to the opportunities provided in technical schools, to the variety of extended courses provided in secondary modern schools, and to the existing arrangements for the transfer of late-maturing pupils from secondary modern schools to grammar schools. A definitive interpretation of the effect of the regional differences in grammar school provision will be reached

[1] Ministry of Education, List 69 (1959).

4

only when it is possible to follow a widely dispersed sample of children throughout their time at school.

As relatively few survey children are at school in the areas of each local education authority, these areas have been grouped into larger geographical regions.[1] In doing this the groupings used by the Registrar General in his analysis of the 1961 census information have been followed. In these large regional areas, there are still great variations in the proportion of survey children who are offered grammar school places.

The regional pattern is little altered when all selective places are taken into account, i.e. when children at independent and technical schools are included with those at grammar schools; and even when the children at comprehensive schools which are not conventionally streamed are added, the regional inequalities persist, and are as follows:

Percentage of Children in Grammar, Technical, Comprehensive and Independent Schools

Region				
Wales	*S. West*	*N. West*	*W. and E. Ridings*	*East*
33·5	35·0	29·5	25·6	24·6

Region				
N. Midland	*Midland*	*London and S. East*	*North*	*South*
26·3	24·1	31·6	22·4	18·9

It seemed possible that some of the inequalities in grammar school allocation might be explained by chance factors which could have led, for example, to a high proportion of middle class

[1] Table IV(*a*), page 144.

children being selected by the survey in some areas and a low one in others. There are indeed great regional differences in the occupations followed by the survey children's fathers, but they are not of the sort to explain the unequal distribution of grammar school places. The largest proportion of semi-skilled and unskilled manual workers' children is in Wales where grammar school places are in good supply; the largest proportion of professional and salaried workers' children is in the South, where there are few places available. By the token of the fathers' occupations, therefore, the existing allocation of places in these two regions should be reversed.

A similar conclusion is reached when we look at the eleven-year test scores: the Welsh children score slightly below the national average,[1] and the children in the South slightly above it. When put into order running from the highest average measured ability to the lowest, Wales comes ninth out of the ten regions and the South comes fifth. These figures plainly give no support for the view that the regions with a high proportion of children at grammar schools have a high average level of ability and those with a low proportion at grammar schools, a low one. There seems indeed to be no consistent relation between the provision of places and the ability of children as measured by us.

There might, of course, be oddities in the distribution of measured ability that would justify the patchy and apparently illogical provision of grammar school places observed in different parts of the country, and we can exclude this possibility only by comparing the allocation of grammar school places in the different regions to children of similar measured ability. This calculation shows that if the existing grammar school places were fairly distributed throughout the country in proportion to the measured ability of the children, the chances of getting a place would be equal (18 per cent) for Welsh children and those in the Southern Region. In fact, 29 per cent of Welsh children go to grammar schools as compared with only 13 per cent of children in the South. Less extreme differences are found between the other regions.[2]

---

[1] The relatively low scores for Wales are based on only 208 children and do not give a reliable measure of the level of national intelligence in that country.

[2] Table IV(*b*), page 145.

The greatest regional differences in the allocation of grammar school places are found among the children whose test scores are at levels (between 52 and 60) where their chances of going to grammar schools are not high. The cleverer children have similar chances in each region. It will be interesting to observe the progress of the children of relatively low measured ability who are admitted in considerable numbers to grammar schools in Wales and the South-West. If they—or a substantial proportion of them—are successful in their studies, it will seem that a national provision of grammar school places for 19 per cent of children is too low and results in a waste of ability. Conversely, if many of these children are academic failures or leave school early, the lower level of grammar school provision in the South will appear more realistic.[1] Some figures of early leaving in the different regions will be found on page 124. They show that a waste of talent through early leaving is especially high in those areas where grammar school places are in short supply.

In each region, both the mothers and the teachers expect more children to go to grammar schools than are actually given places, and there is a rough similarity in their views which suggests that, as more places are provided, so expectations rise.[2]

The next problem to consider is the relation between internal migration and regional inequalities in secondary school provision. Much has been written about the effects of population movements on the distribution of intelligence. When the main direction of movement was from the rural areas to the towns, and from the small towns to the larger ones, it seemed that the towns were attracting the more able and go-ahead people from the surrounding country areas, which were correspondingly depleted of talent. Further away beyond the pull of the towns the population was not depleted. The pattern found, for example, in Northumberland in the 1920s was of a high level of ability among school children near cities and far away from them, and of a low level of ability in the intermediate areas, 'as if they had been emptied of the more able members by the attractions of the towns with

---

[1] In making these assessments, the provision of extended courses in secondary modern schools and the later transfer of pupils to grammar schools will have to be taken into account.

[2] Table IV(*b*), page 145.

their more favourable opportunities for social advancement'.[1] It was not of course always the more intelligent that were attracted to the towns, and if the demand was for unskilled labour the villages from which it was recruited had a disproportionate number of bright children: the sons and daughters of those who, not being attracted by unskilled employment, were left behind. But this type of change was the exception.

Sixty-seven per cent of the children in this study moved their homes at least once during the eleven years covered by this report, and 23 per cent moved on more than one occasion.[2] Moves were most frequent during the early years of the survey when many of the parents were young and unencumbered by large families and when they were adjusting to the extensive social changes of the late forties. But even at the present time moves are by no means infrequent and between 1953 and 1957, while these children were at primary schools, 32 per cent moved house once or more often.

The majority of these moves were over short distances, often into council houses in the same village or town, and between 1946 and 1957 only 12 per cent of families moved further than nineteen miles. The more distant moves were made predominantly by middle class families, particularly those where the husband was in a profession. These, in spite of their small number, might give rise to a considerable geographical redistribution of ability if they were canalised in one direction only; if for example there had been a general move to London and the South, where the number of grammar school places, already in short supply, would become more so owing to an influx of children of high ability. There is, however, no marked trend of this sort, a slight increase since 1946 in the proportion of middle class families living in London and the South having been followed by only a very slight increase in the competition for grammar school places there.

When the average test performance of children in families which have never moved is compared with the performance of those in families that have moved, it is found that the former make lower average scores in the tests than the latter, but the average test score for each region is little altered because the children who move in have approximately the same superior ability as those who move out. The only considerable changes are in the South-West where the average level of ability, as measured at eleven, increases owing to migration by 0·42 points, the East where it increases by 0·39 points and the North Midlands where it decreases by 0·55 points.[1] (None of these differences exceeds those expected by chance.)

This is the only evidence to suggest that families with more able children are being attracted to certain regions of the country, while other regions are being depleted of talent. It may be concluded, then, that the movement of families from one part of the country to another does not present any serious problem of secondary selection, at any rate when the position is considered on a regional basis. In an individual authority, however, the development of a new industry attracting highly skilled workers and technicians may well increase the competition for grammar school places and, until the necessary adjustments in school provision have been made, may result in the exclusion of able children from these schools who in other circumstances would have secured places. Unfortunately the size of this sample is such that we cannot study important local problems of this sort.

Another aspect of migration is conveniently considered here, though it is only distantly related to regional inequalities in educational opportunity. How is the performance of children at school influenced by moving? It might be influenced by the dislocation of study resulting from frequent changes of school, or more remotely, by emotional disturbances having their origins in early childhood and stemming from the insecurity of small children when suddenly moved from a familiar home environment to a new and unknown one.

The children who moved while they were at primary school are in no way at a disadvantage as compared with those who remained in the same home and the same school; they show the same changes in school performance between eight and eleven years and, in relation to their measured ability, stand just as good a chance of going to grammar schools. This is the overall picture:

[1] Table IV(c), page 146.

it is blurred because we do not have a description of all the primary schools attended but only of those the children were going to when they were eleven years old. It is possible that some children may have suffered by changing from schools with good teaching to schools with poor, but if so this has been fully compensated for by those who moved conversely. It may be, of course, that children who are trying to adjust to new schools and new teachers—and also at the same time to new homes and the problems of finding new friends—have temporary difficulties with their work. We can only compare their performances at eight and eleven, and from this viewpoint such temporary difficulties do not show themselves.

There is a common belief that frequent changes of home in early childhood are associated with behaviour problems such as bed-wetting, nightmares and temper tantrums. It seemed worthwhile, therefore, to look at the children who had moved home several times in the pre-school years but not later, and see whether there was evidence of any effect on their school work.

Children who have moved house several times during the first five years of their lives make lower scores in the eight-year tests than those who have not moved or moved only once in the preschool years, and they are still behind the latter, though less so, at eleven.[1] However, there may well be subtle factors of selection to be considered when assessing these families who moved frequently during the first five years of the survey, and I do not wish to over-emphasise this finding.

The conclusions of this chapter may be summarised as follows. Regional differences in the provision of grammar school places in no way reflect real differences in the ability of the children or in the availability of private schools. Even the best selection procedure will fail to make full use of the available talent of children so long as there is a shortage of grammar school places in some areas and not in others.

Internal movements of the population do not add materially to the discrepancy between the regional distribution of ability and of grammar school places. But within smaller areas than we have been able to examine, a fixed number of places will not always be sufficient since a relatively small change in the social

[1] Table IV(d), page 146.

composition of the families in an area, such as might result from an influx of those engaged in skilled trades or clerical work, may lead to large swings in the intensity of competition for the available grammar school places. The level of ability needed to qualify for a place will then rise unless, of course, the number of places is correspondingly increased.

Other aspects of internal migration have been looked at. We find that school progress is not affected by frequent moves during the primary school period, but that children do less well in the tests if they have a history of frequent moves in early childhood; between eight and eleven years, however, they catch up to some extent.

CHAPTER V

The Homes

THE following chapters describe the influence of the homes and schools on educational opportunity in England and Wales today. There is a danger that by concentrating attention on the methods used to select children for secondary education, we may fail to appreciate the importance of other ways in which talent is lost or diverted. A study of the measured ability of children in relation to their admission to grammar or secondary modern schools does not necessarily give the full picture of educational waste. If the standards of grammar school selection are set too high, there will be waste that is no less undesirable because it is spread over the social classes. If a child's ability at eleven years gives only a poor prediction of his ability at later ages, there will also be waste. At an even earlier age, waste of talent may occur through the effects of an adverse home environment or through lack of stimulation in early life or at school.

When considering the relation between environment and educational opportunity, I recognise that innate endowment may well be the most powerful influence in determining the level of achievement at school. But even if outside factors such as the parents' interest and encouragement, home circumstances, or the quality of teaching, have only a small effect on performance, their combined action may lead to a considerable waste of talent owing to the exclusion from grammar schools of children who, given other homes or other schools, would have succeeded in getting there. There is evidence that extreme poverty of the environment (such as surrounded mill children in North Carolina, or canal boat children in England), leads to a progressive deterioration in academic ability.[1] At the other extreme, some families have a tradition of making the best use of their brains and their lives and this may depend more on methods of upbringing than on inherited traits. In such families the children

[1] Jordan, A. M. (1933).
  Neff, W. S. (1938).

31

are stimulated in numerous ways and are kept busy playing games that demand thought, and so from their earliest years acquire a totally different attitude to learning. I am not, of course, talking here only of 'innate' intelligence, but of the ability to succeed in school studies, which requires qualities of will and continuity of effort. Failure to acquire these will lead to a waste of ability that no redistribution of grammar school places or refinements of 11+ selection can avoid.

During the eleven years of this survey home circumstances improved greatly. Thirty per cent of middle class families moved to houses with better amenities than those they started with and only 7 per cent moved to worse. This was largely owing to the purchase of new homes which in general offered more space and better amenities than the houses and flats rented from private landlords when the survey started. Whereas 39 per cent of middle class families owned their homes in 1946, 58 per cent did so in 1957. During this period overcrowding[1] decreased from 7 per cent to 3 per cent.

There has been an even greater improvement in the housing of manual working class families, though a large number of them are still living in circumstances that are far from satisfactory. House purchase played only a small part in this improvement, which was largely brought about by the provision of council houses and flats. Nearly twice as many manual working class families are living on council estates today as at the beginning of the survey and their homes, though sometimes small in size, provide the modern amenities that were often lacking in the privately rented accommodation they left. Forty-six per cent of these families are now living in council houses and 62 per cent have their own kitchen and bathroom as well as running hot water. There is a substantial improvement in the amenities enjoyed by 44 per cent of them and the amount of overcrowding has been halved. This encouraging picture of working-class housing is offset by the fact that 22 per cent still share a bathroom or kitchen and have no running hot water, and 13 per cent have at least two persons to every habitable room in the house.

Not all the families improved their housing conditions; 7 per

---

[1] A house is 'overcrowded' if there are two or more persons to each room, counting the kitchen if used as a living room.

cent are living in homes that are less well equipped than those they had eleven years ago. The reason is sometimes prolonged unemployment, mainly through illness, and sometimes the break-up of families owing to death, divorce or separation. In these circumstances, families move into cheaper dwellings or to relatives, and such moves usually result in an acute deterioration of amenities and an increase in the number of persons per room.

Moves to council houses provided the most important source of improved living conditions for the manual working classes. How have these moves affected their children's progress at school and their chances in the 11+ selection examinations? It has been noted in Middlesbrough[1] that when families moved from the slums to council estates their children's chances of going to grammar schools were increased. These children may have done better at school because their health improved or because they tried harder when they came into an area where education was valued. Alternatively, there may have been more grammar school places available in these new areas and less competition for them.

The allocation of families to council houses is, of course, not done at random and those given the opportunity to rent them tend to be among the educationally least promising families of any in this sample. They come predominantly from the lower manual working classes; they tend to have many children and, according to the health visitors, look after them badly in the sense that many do not accept immunisation when it is offered them, and fail to make use of the ante- and post-natal services which are provided. Their children also have a lower measured ability than manual working class children in general; they show a deterioration in test scores between eight and eleven years, but this is less than the deterioration recorded for those who continued to rent their homes from private landlords throughout the whole survey period.

When manual working class children who live on council estates are compared with all children from this class, we find that they get 10 per cent more places in grammar schools than would be expected from their measured ability, whereas those who live in homes rented from private landlords get 11 per cent

[1] Glass, R. (1948). It was because of this survey that Middlesbrough was one of the areas chosen by Floud, Halsey and Martin.

fewer. Similar differences are found in all parts of the country. As the following table shows, the advantage enjoyed by the council estate children is particularly marked for the brighter ones.

Level of test score at eleven	Living throughout on Council Estates	Moving to Council Estates	Living throughout in Private Dwellings
	% at Grammar School	% at Grammar School	% at Grammar School
61 and over	98·3	88·5	75·0
58–60	51·4	43·9	38·7
55–57	28·9	19·8	15·0
49–54	4·0	5·3	4·7

There is no suggestion from the teachers that the children who lived throughout on council estates, or recently moved to them, work any harder than those living in houses rented from private landlords. Nor is there any reason to believe that parents who live on council estates are more ambitious for their children to succeed at school; those who live in privately rented houses express similar views on school leaving and show no substantial difference in their level of interest in their children's studies. It seems, then, that the greater educational opportunities of the children who live on council estates arise from a more liberal provision of grammar school places, rather than from a direct influence of improved housing on educational progress.

The next question to consider is whether children who are brought up in houses with plenty of living space and good amenities show any benefit in their progress at school or in the results of the secondary selection examinations. The homes are classified by whether or not they are overcrowded, by whether the survey children share their beds or sleep alone, and by whether there is running hot water and a kitchen and bathroom that is not shared with another family. These are, of course, closely related conditions. Children who share their beds usually, but not always, live in overcrowded homes. The best amenities are found in the most modern houses which are usually, but not always, the least crowded. Preliminary tables showed that the sharing of beds, overcrowding and lack of household amenities each influence the performance of children to a similar extent and in the same direction, and so these measures have been combined to describe two types of home; first, those in which not more than one adverse rating on crowding, bed-sharing or lack of amenities was recorded and, second, those in which two or more adverse ratings were recorded.[1]

This simple division of children into those who live in 'satisfactory' and 'unsatisfactory' homes, yields groups which in each social class are of different measured ability.[2]

From the studies of mill and canal boat children referred to at the beginning of this chapter, it seemed probable that an impoverished home environment would have a cumulative effect, so that the children exposed to it would become progressively more handicapped in their test performance as they grew older. For the manual working class children this is indeed so; those whose homes are unsatisfactory make lower scores in the eleven-year tests than in the eight-year tests, losing an average of 0·66 points of score during these three years, whereas those from satisfactory homes improve their score during the same period by an average of 0·04 points.

In the middle classes the position is reversed, that is to say the children from unsatisfactory homes, far from deteriorating in performance between eight and eleven years, make up part of their earlier handicap. In these social classes it seems that overcrowding, the sharing of beds and poor home circumstances have exerted their full effect by eight years, if not earlier, and that their influence is offset by other favourable factors in the homes or in the schools.

The assessment of the environment in which these children grew up is made from a mass of information gathered over eleven years by health visitors, school nurses and teachers. We know, among other things, about the houses in which the children lived, the social background and education of their parents, the

[1] Table V(a), page 147.
[2] Table V(b), page 148.

views of their mothers on their education, the size of the families they belonged to and the academic record and characteristics of the schools they attended. All these environmental aspects are, of course, overlapping in their effects; parents who are unskilled workers, for example, will often be of low educational attainment, take little interest in their children's school-work, have large families, live in grossly overcrowded homes lacking amenities (unless they are fortunate enough to have a council house) and may well send their children to primary schools which are ill-equipped, with large classes and less than first-rate teaching. It is important, then, that no firm conclusions on the influence of any one aspect of the environment should be reached until all have been considered together.

The analysis made by H. R. Simpson at Rothamsted (see Appendix II, page 133) allows the influence of housing to be separated from the overlapping effects of family size, parents' interest, and the academic record of the school. When this is done the first crude estimate of the extent to which the standard of housing influences the average level of test score is somewhat reduced, though the difference between its influence on middle-class and manual working class children is enhanced. The adjusted average test scores[1] for middle class children, even more clearly than the crude scores, show that those who live in the least satisfactory type of home start off with a handicap in their test scores at eight which they reduce substantially during the next three years; the middle class girls it seems are more successful than the boys in reducing this handicap. Further, the adjusted average scores for the manual working class children show again more clearly than the crude scores that those in poor home circumstances not only do badly in the eight-year tests, but deteriorate in test performance during the next three years.

The importance of the influence of housing on measured ability is indicated by the statistical levels of significance recorded in this analysis, and it is evident (see Appendix II, page 138) that, as they grow older, the performance of middle class children is less influenced, whereas that of manual working class children is more influenced by the sort of homes they come from.

[1] i.e. the scores after allowances have been made for the effects of family size, parents' interest and the academic record of the school.

The teachers say that the children from unsatisfactory homes tend to be poor workers or lazy and that the manual working class children from these homes have poor powers of concentration in school. They also consider that children from unsatisfactory homes are less able to profit from grammar school education than children from satisfactory ones, and they say this even when they are comparing children of the same measured ability. Perhaps their views reflect the attitudes of the parents themselves who, when home conditions are unsatisfactory, tend to have low educational ambitions, to wish their children to leave school early and, in the manual working classes, to expect them to go to secondary modern rather than to grammar schools.

When children of similar measured ability compete for grammar school places, those from satisfactory homes have an advantage over the rest which, though small, is consistent in each social class, whether the area be one of good or poor provision of grammar school places.[1] (This finding, however, though in the expected direction, does not reach a level of statistical significance in any social class.)

There are many possible explanations for the deterioration observed between eight and eleven years in the test performance of children whose home circumstances are bad. In overcrowded homes they will be deprived of quiet and privacy. When they share their beds they may sleep badly, and through tiredness, be unable to concentrate on their school work. But such explanations do not account for the observed difference between the educational progress of middle and manual working class children. If overcrowding, bad sleeping habits, and lack of amenities are associated with deterioration in the test performance of manual working class children, why are they not equally associated with a deterioration in the progress of middle class children?

Middle class parents are likely to provide some privacy for their children even if their homes are unsatisfactory, whereas similarly placed working class parents fail to do this. But there may be more to it than this. Perhaps it is the type of area rather than the standard of housing that is important. Middle class children, even if their home circumstances are bad, are likely to

[1] Table V(c), page 149.

mix with other middle class children who come from families where education is valued. In contrast manual working class children in similarly substandard homes will often live in poor neighbourhoods where there is little interest in learning, so that both they and their parents may be discouraged by the apathy and disinterest around them. Unfortunately since our information concerns households and not neighbourhoods we cannot look further into this question.

This chapter may be summarised as follows. For any given level of measured ability children living on council estates have better chances of going to grammar schools than those who live in privately rented dwellings. This appears to be explained by the better provision of grammar school places in these new areas rather than by any special qualities of the children or the sharpened aspirations of their parents. When housing conditions are unsatisfactory, children make relatively low scores in the tests. This is so in each social class but whereas the middle class children, as they get older, reduce this handicap, the manual working class children from unsatisfactory homes fall even further behind; for them, overcrowding and other deficiencies at home have a progressive and depressive influence on their test performance.

CHAPTER VI

The Parents

EVEN in early infancy contacts between children and parents may influence later educational achievement by establishing a wish to learn. 'The child whose memories are associated with resentment cannot be expected to compete successfully with those whose memories are associated with a feeling of what we call personal satisfaction or a sense of achievement.'[1] There is much evidence to show that the care of intelligent and understanding parents in the early years gives background and meaning to what is learned.

In this study we have no direct knowledge of the early influence of parents on their children's attitudes to learning, and can infer this only from what is known of their social origins and education, and of the level of skill they attain in their jobs. When, in an earlier book,[2] the growth and health of these children was described, a social classification was used that was based on their fathers' jobs alone. They were divided into nine 'occupational groups', ranging from the children of professional workers to the children of unskilled labourers. There were wide differences in the amount of illness, and rate of growth, among these nine groups of children, also in the use that their parents made of the medical services. The main distinction lies between the children of the non-manual workers and those of the manual workers. The former have, on the average, relatively little infectious illness in early childhood, they enjoy excellent standards of care at home and their mothers take them regularly to the child welfare centres and in general make good use of the available medical services. They have in other words what may be regarded as a middle class pattern of upbringing. In contrast, the manual working class children are more often ill, particularly with respiratory tract infections, and their mothers are seen by the health visitors as giving low standards of care to their children and homes, as

[1] Russell, W. R. (1957).
[2] Douglas, J. W. B., and Blomfield, J. M. (1958), p. 29.
5

making relatively little use of the child welfare centres and as often failing to have their children immunised against diphtheria.

It was originally intended to use the same nine occupational groups in this educational study. It soon became clear, however, that these groups were fluctuating and ill-defined. Some of this instability arose from the difficulty of establishing with accuracy the degree of skill used in particular jobs; job descriptions were often imprecise in spite of checking, and sometimes grossly misleading, so that in the light of further information 12 per cent of the original job codings had to be altered. But apart from this, job changes were frequent, and over the eleven years of this survey 43 per cent of families moved out of their original occupational groups, and some passed through several different groups.

This large volume of occupational movement stems in part from the relatively large number of groups into which the families were divided; there were nine groups instead of the five which the Registrar General uses routinely in his analyses of mortality. The greatest amount of change, however, is among the manual workers, who frequently move from semi-skilled to skilled occupations or vice versa; and so even the Registrar General's classification, which is largely based on the criterion of skill, would turn out to be fluctuating and impermanent when applied to a longitudinal study of this kind.

The survey started soon after the war and it might be thought that the greater part of the changes in employment that were recorded would be in the immediately succeeding years and represent an adjustment to peace-time conditions, but this was not so. The amount of change between the nine groups used at the beginning of this study was relatively steady from year to year, at a level of approximately 6 per cent. Some groups, for example professional or salaried workers, become more stable as time passes, recruiting from the younger men and losing mainly through retirement. Others, for example the black-coated wage earners or agricultural workers, show an even greater rate of change at the end of the survey than at the beginning. The main direction of change is upward, but there is a semi-permeable barrier between the non-manual and the manual groups across which, during the whole eleven years, only 5 per cent moved up and 3 per cent down.

Before going further with this discussion of how to classify these families we shall look at the unemployed; these are few in number but important because of the state of poverty in which they live and the signs of deprivation in their children. Unemployment among the fathers was 0·9 per cent in 1950,[1] increasing to 2·9 per cent in 1957. Virtually all prolonged unemployment was a result of mental or physical illness or handicap, and the families were often profoundly affected. They lived in the most unsuitable and overcrowded homes, showed many other signs of poverty and were usually supported by the wages earned by the wives, who worked for long hours away from their homes and children.

Since these fathers were unemployed because they were ill rather than because they were mentally dull there is no reason why their children should do worse in the tests and in the secondary selection examinations than other children coming from similarly deprived homes. There is here no special element of inherited subnormality to take into account. But in fact they do considerably worse; they make an average score at eight years of 44·38 and, at eleven, of 44·47. These compare with average scores of 46·88 and 46·00 for the children of unskilled labourers at these ages. Seven per cent of the unskilled labourers' children go to grammar schools as compared with only 3 per cent of the children of the unemployed, and the teachers report that the latter are lazy and inattentive in school and that their parents take little interest in their progress. It may be that the key to their backwardness lies in worries and anxieties at home.

Families that move up or down the social scale have the characteristics and aspirations of the group they are joining rather than of the one they have left; this holds also for the ability of their children as measured by our tests and the results of the 11 + examinations. Children in families that are moving up have higher measured ability than those they leave behind though rather less than those they join. They also improve their test scores between the ages of eight and eleven years and if this improvement is maintained will soon eliminate their present slight handicap in the group they have joined. The reverse is true for the children in families that have moved down.

[1] 1950 was the first year for which this information is available.

It seems, then, that the occupational changes of the eleven years of this survey have reshuffled the families by the social origins and education of the parents and, at second remove, by the intelligence of their children. It is likely that this process will continue in future years, and for this reason alone the father's occupation is an unsatisfactory criterion of social status for our present purpose. There is considerable sociological interest in observing the extent of movement between occupations, but this is not the main aim of this study—we wish to have a more stable means of summarising the social status of the families, which will also enable us to group together families of similar aspirations and standards.

The instability of occupations is not the only reason for abandoning them as a criterion of social status. It is, of course, inconvenient to have social categories that fluctuate and contain, at any chosen time, many families destined to move up or down and already showing some of the characteristics of the social group they will eventually join. This can only blur social differences. In addition, however, the boundaries of the categories are ill-defined and become more so as methods of payment— which allow salaried workers to be distinguished from clerical wage earners—change. An occupational classification can also be misleading in other ways; for example, there are in this survey several manual workers whose occupations give an entirely false impression of the opportunities of their children who are maintained at boarding schools by grandparents or godfathers.[1]

A further serious criticism of a purely occupational classification is that it applies only to the fathers. We cannot afford to ignore the background of the mothers when looking at the educational progress of their children; they make an equal contribution with the fathers to inherited ability and possibly a greater one to attitudes to learning. In ambitious working class households it is not unusual to find that the mother comes from a middle class family and supplies the drive and incentive for her children to do well at school.

The education of both the parents is known and also the types of family in which they were each brought up. We will

---

[1] One of these for example was a teacher who after a nervous breakdown became a gardener.

now see how far the social background and education of each
parent relates to the views expressed by the mothers on their
children's education. As our contacts were solely with the
mothers it might be expected that the views they expressed
would be more closely associated with their own education and
origins than with their husbands'. This, however, was not so; the
views expressed, for example, by mothers brought up in working-
class families and educated at elementary schools, who were
married to men with middle-class origins and secondary education, were exactly the same as those expressed by mothers
with middle class origins and secondary education who were
married to men brought up in working-class families and
educated at elementary schools. Each group wanted their
children on the average to leave school at sixteen years and eight
months and each showed the same level of interest in their
children's school progress. Moreover the level of their aspirations
fell exactly between those of the two most contrasting groups;
namely parents with entirely middle-class origins and secondary
education on the one hand and those with entirely working-class
origins and elementary education on the other.

The influence of the mothers' education and social backgrounds
is also evident when we look at the average test scores of their
children and performance in the secondary selection examinations; this influence is as strong as that of the fathers' education
and social backgrounds, but no stronger. We know that for many
young children it is the early contacts with their mothers that are
likely to have the greatest influence on learning, and at later ages,
too, it is often the mother who is more concerned than the father
with school problems, and has the closest contact with the
teachers. Because of this it seemed that among the survey children the mothers' influence on performance in school and in the
tests might transcend the fathers'. That it exerts no more than
an equal influence may perhaps be explained by the tendency for
people to marry those with similar standards and ambitions. At
any rate these observations show that it would be unwise to
ignore the social origins and standard of education of the mothers
when devising a new social classification.

The families were then grouped in the following way. First,
those with a predominantly 'middle class' background, that is to

say one of the parents was brought up in a non-manual worker's family *and* went to a secondary school, and the other had at least one of these characteristics; second, those with a purely working-class background, where both parents came from manual workers' families and received only an elementary school education; third, those who showed some middle class characteristics but did not fit into the first group.

When these three classes of families are further divided by the nature of the husband's present occupation a clear picture emerges.[1] The children of non-manual workers fall into two main groups which have considerably different average scores in the eight- and eleven-year tests: those whose parents have middle class origins and secondary school education form a group which, on the average, make high scores whether their fathers are in the professions, in salaried employment, in blackcoated work or are self-employed; the remainder, whose parents may be said to deviate in their upbringing and education from the middle class pattern, make considerably lower average scores. The children from the first group not only make relatively high scores in the eight- and eleven-year tests, but also work hard in class and do conspicuously well in the 11+ examinations, getting more grammar school places than would be expected from their measured ability. In contrast, those from the second group, whose parents deviate from the middle class pattern, are less interested in their work and do relatively less well in the 11+ examinations. These differences in the performance of the children are reflected in the interests and aspirations of their parents. For these reasons the non-manual workers are grouped into two classes, the 'upper middle class' and the 'lower middle class'. Upper class and lower class are phrases we dislike, but in practice they give a convenient short description of these two groups. In making this division the employers and the self-employed are treated in the same way as the rest of the non-manual workers.

The manual working class families also split naturally into two groups. First, those in which one or both parents come from a middle class family, or have been to secondary schools. The great

---

[1] A paper giving a detailed account of the social characteristics of this sample is being prepared for publication.

majority of these are skilled workers and we call them the 'upper manual working class'. Second, those in which both parents were brought up in working class families and had only an elementary school education; these we call the 'lower manual working class'. The latter may be regarded as wholly manual working class in origin, whereas the upper manual working class families deviate from this pattern. The lower manual working class children consistently show a substantial decline in test scores between eight and eleven years, and this is so whether the father is in skilled, semi-skilled or unskilled employment.

This division into four social classes[1] (the upper and lower middle classes and the upper and lower manual working classes) has the great virtue for this study that it provides relatively stable groups that include essentially the same families whether the classification is made on the information available at the beginning of the survey or the end of it. Some assessments of these families are given in the following table. The home circumstances and the primary schools attended by these children are described in Tables VI(b) and (c) on pages 150 and 151.

	Middle Class Mothers		Manual Working Class Mothers	
	Upper	Lower	Upper	Lower
	%	%	%	%
Highest standards of infant care	53·1	37·0	22·1	15·1
Highest standards of infant management	66·2	49·4	34·5	28·1
Good use of medical services	78·9	67·4	54·2	42·4
High interest in school progress	41·7	21·7	11·4	5·0
Desires grammar school place[2]	73·3	73·3	57·7	48·8
Late school leaving wished	77·6	40·7	21·7	12·9
At least four of the above	81·0	58·0	34·6	19·6

There are considerable differences, as mentioned already, in the average test scores made by children in these four social

[1] Table VI(a) page 150 gives the number of children in each social class.
[2] Irrespective of leaving age desired.

classes.[1] The upper middle class children, at eleven years, make an average score of 56·99; the lower middle class 53·88; the upper manual working class 50·05; the lower manual working class 47·55. It might be thought that the social class differences in test performance would be greatest in the tests which measured the level of achievement in school subjects, but this is not so. There are similar differences between the social classes in each type of test that was used, and a slight suggestion that the lower manual working class children are under-achievers and that the upper middle class children are over-achievers.[2] The intelligence test used at eleven years was in two parts, one of which was given pictorially (and so did not involve the understanding of words), whereas the other involved seeing similarities between the meanings of words. There is a very slight tendency for the middle class children to do better in the 'verbal' than in the 'non-verbal' part of this intelligence test, whereas the manual working class children do worse in the 'verbal' part. This is mentioned because it confirms the findings of some other studies, but standing alone it might well be explained as a chance effect because the differences are so slight.

At eleven years the average test scores made by children in the four social classes differ more widely than they did at eight. The two middle class groups come closer together and move further away from the manual working classes; this shows itself in intelligence tests as well as in tests of school achievement.

It is well known that when tests are repeated after an interval, children who make low scores tend, on the average, to improve their position, whereas those who make high scores tend to deteriorate. It would therefore be expected that the middle class children who, on the average, score highly at eight would show a drop in score at eleven, and that the manual working class children who make low scores at eight would show an improvement; but, as has already been mentioned, the middle class children improve their scores and the working class children deteriorate—this holds at each level of ability. By the time he is eleven, the clever manual working class child has fallen behind the middle class child of similar ability at eight years, and

[1] Table VI(d), page 151.
[2] Table VI(e), page 152.

equally the backward manual working class child shows less improvement between eight and eleven years than the backward middle class child. The consistency of these differences is shown in the following table.

| Score at eight years | Middle Class | | Manual Working Class | |
| | Upper | Lower | Upper | Lower |
	Change in score 8–11 years	Change in score 8–11 years	Change in score 8–11 years	Change in score 8–11 years
40 or below	*	+2·52	+0·50	+0·68
41–45	*	+1·84	+0·90	— ·23
46–50	+3·44	+2·38	+0·59	+0·02
51–55	+1·81	+1·71	+0·19	—0·78
56–60	+1·52	+0·62	—0·81	—2·27
60 and over	—2·32	—1·94	—3·17	—4·60

* Fewer than 20 children in these groups

+ = improvement   — = deterioration

Social class differences in secondary selection are marked. Fifty-four per cent of upper middle class children, but only 11 per cent of lower manual working class children, go to grammar schools; and not all of the poor achievement of the working class children is explained by their lower measured ability. If we compare secondary selection within groups of children whose eleven-year test scores are similar, the middle class children are consistently at an advantage until very high levels of performance are reached. With children in the top two per cent of ability, social background is unimportant, but below this it has a considerable influence on their chances of going to grammar schools. As an illustration consider children who score between 55 and 57 in the tests; among them grammar school places are awarded at the age of eleven to 51 per cent from the upper middle classes, 34 per cent from the lower middle, 21 per cent from the upper manual, and 22 per cent from the lower manual working classes.[1]

The reason for these differences may lie in the personal qualities of the pupils (their industry and behaviour in class) or in the attitude of their parents, who may give them much or little encouragement in their work. At the present time these inequalities may be inevitable; but they still result in a considerable waste of ability which may be conserved in the future when attitudes to education have changed. It is not an idle exercise to work out how many grammar school places would be needed if the opportunities for selection which are enjoyed by upper middle class children applied to the population at large.

If at each level of measured ability at eleven all children, whatever their home background, had the same chance of getting to grammar school as the upper middle class children, places would be needed for 27 per cent of children rather than for 21 per cent.[2]

In the regions where there is relatively good provision of grammar school places, the lower middle class children do just as well for each level of measured ability as the upper middle class in the selection examinations. In contrast the upper manual working class children get 15 per cent fewer places in grammar schools than would be got by a group of upper middle class children with a similar distribution of test scores, and the lower manual working class children get 28 per cent fewer. It is particularly the children of just above average ability who are at a disadvantage.

When grammar school places are in short supply the upper middle class children are as likely to get grammar school places as they would be if they lived in more favoured regions. The main effect of the shortage falls on the lower middle and the manual working class children. The lower middle class children living in these poorly favoured areas get 28 per cent fewer places than an equivalent group of upper middle class children, the upper manual working class children get 40 per cent fewer, and the lower manual working class children get 48 per cent fewer. Among the latter even the relatively clever children—with scores

[1] In Chapter XV and Table XV(a), page 179, the corresponding figures refer to the position at fifteen years.
[2] Of those competing for grammar school places.

of 61 and over—get 15 per cent fewer places than an equivalent group of upper middle class children. It seems that when grammar school places are hard to come by, it is particularly the manual working class child who is affected.[1]

Grammar school awards are of course seldom made on the results of intelligence tests and school achievement tests alone. A director of education might think it unjustifiable to send a relatively able child to a grammar school if his chances of success were small through lack of staying power and ambition. And this view is especially likely when the available number of grammar school places is strictly limited. Perhaps manual working class children fail to get the number of grammar school places that their measured ability would justify, because many of them lack these and other qualities needed for later academic success; qualities, moreover, which our relatively short and specialised tests do not measure. This explanation is untenable in face of the regional differences that have just been described, unless one is prepared to accept that the staying power and ambition of working class children varies from one part of the country to another and is at its lowest in just those areas where grammar school places are in short supply. This is improbable to say the least.

If the eight-year tests, rather than the eleven-year tests, are taken as the criterion of ability, the manual working class children are at a considerably greater disadvantage.

It was estimated on page 48 that if all children were to be given the opportunities enjoyed by the upper middle class children of similar ability at eleven, the provision of grammar school places would have to be increased from 21 per cent to 27 per cent. When ability is measured by the eight-year tests, it may be estimated in the same way that the provision of places would have to be increased to 33 per cent.

How realistic are these figures? In the long run we shall have to judge this by seeing what happens to children in the grammar schools of Wales and the South-West, where the intake is already at this high level.

But an immediate indication of whether this estimate is unrealistic is given by the teachers' views on their pupils' ability

[1] Table VI(f), page 153.

to profit from a grammar school type of education; these fit closely with the estimates which were made on the basis of performance in the eleven-year tests. In the upper manual working class, for example, the teachers say that 28 per cent of the children should go to grammar schools as compared with 26 per cent estimated from the results of the tests.[1] In the lower manual working class the equivalent figures are 17 per cent and 18 per cent. The close correspondence between the views of the teachers and the estimates based on the eleven-year tests are echoed by the aspirations of the parents. Thirty per cent of the upper manual working class parents and 22 per cent of the lower manual working class parents hope that their children will go to grammar schools and stay there until they are seventeen at least.[2] The evidence of this study, then, points to there being a shortage of grammar school places. Owing to this, able working class children with parents who are willing to let them profit from a grammar school education are being deprived of the opportunity.

One other attribute of the parents should be discussed here— their age. This has a practical value in interpreting attitudes to education. Each year more parents encourage their children to stay on at school after fifteen. Does this reflect the attitude of the younger parents who, having themselves stayed on at school, are more ambitious for their children; or is it explained by more general influences? Perhaps parents of all ages are becoming more aware of the value of education in modern society, or perhaps more of them today can allow their children to stay on at school after fifteen. Some of the parents in this study were at school in the first world war and others in the second, so that there are in the same sample widely separated generations. Yet no consistent differences are found. In the upper middle classes the oldest fathers would keep their children longest at school, in the other classes the youngest would do so. In no instance was there on the average a difference of more than three months between the views of the oldest and youngest parents. It seems that similar attitudes to education are shown by parents of all ages, and that the secular trend towards later

[1] If at each level of ability at eleven years they had the same opportunity as all upper middle class children of similar ability.

[2] Table VI(g), page 154.

school-leaving is a result of a general change affecting all parents and not only the younger ones.

In conclusion, it will not have escaped notice that the lower manual working class children are doubly handicapped. Their performance in the tests of mental ability and school achievement shows a relative decline between eight and eleven years, and their chances of going to grammar school are low even when allowance is made for the level of their measured ability at the time of the selection examinations. We see in the next chapter how this double handicap is related to the level of the parents' interest in their children's progress at school.

CHAPTER VII

Parental Encouragement

SOCIAL class, as defined in the last chapter, summarises many different aspects of the home environment. We now look at the extent to which parents take an interest in their children's work at school and encourage them to succeed. The aim of this chapter is to see how the performance of children in the tests and in the secondary selection examinations is influenced by the attitudes of their parents, and the encouragement they receive at home.

A rough measure of the mothers' educational aspirations was given in Chapter III by separating those who wished their children to go to grammar schools and stay there until they were more than sixteen years old, from those who were educationally less ambitious. The mothers' attitudes, even when measured in this rough way, have an important influence on their children's chances of getting grammar school places (see page 21). But parents may give support and encouragement to their children even though they realise that they are not clever enough to stand a chance of getting a place in a grammar school. A more generally applicable measure of educational interest is needed, which moreover, takes account of the attitudes of both parents and not of the mother alone.

The middle class parents take more interest in their children's progress at school than the manual working class parents do, and they become relatively more interested as their children grow older. They visit the schools more frequently to find out how their children are getting on with their work, and when they do so are more likely to ask to see the Head as well as the class teacher, whereas the manual working class parents are usually content to see the class teacher only. But the most striking difference is that many middle class fathers visit the schools to discuss their children's progress whereas manual working class fathers seldom do so. (Thirty-two per cent of middle class fathers visit the schools, but only 12 per cent of manual working class fathers.) The teachers' contacts with the working class families are largely through the mothers, and this may explain why they become relatively less frequent as the children get older, whereas with the middle classes they become more frequent. The working class mothers have a particular interest in seeing how their children settle in when they first go to school, but may feel diffident about discussing their educational progress with the teachers at a later stage; and it seems either that their husbands are not prepared to take on this responsibility, or that they are unable to do so owing to the difficulty of taking time off work to visit the schools.

The parents who make frequent visits to the schools and are seen by the teachers as very interested in their children's education are also outstanding in the use they make of the available medical services. They seldom fail to bring their children to the child welfare centres or have them immunised against diphtheria and other diseases and they are regarded by the health visitors as giving a high standard of care to their children and homes. Their children benefit not only from the support and encouragement they get in their school work but also from the excellent personal and medical care they enjoy at home.

In contrast, the parents who seldom visit the schools and seem to the teachers to be uninterested in their children's progress make little use of the available medical services, often fail to take their children to the welfare centres or to have them immunised and, according to the health visitors, often neglect their homes and give their children low standards of care. There is a greater amount of illness and school absence among their children, whose work suffers to some extent from this[1] as well as from their parents' lack of interest in their educational progress. Perhaps this extra burden of illness explains why these parents worry about their children's health and behaviour more than the other parents. These worries may be partly justified, but one carries away a picture of a group of mothers who are worrying about their children without taking the steps necessary to put things right.

In this study, the level of the parents' interest in their children's work was partly based on comments made by the class teachers at the end of the first and at the end of the fourth primary school year, and partly on the records of the number of times

[1] A paper on school absence is being prepared for separate publication.

each parent visited the schools to discuss their child's progress with the Head or class teacher. Parents are said to show a 'high level of interest' if the teachers regarded them throughout the primary school period as very interested in their children's work and if they had also taken the opportunity to visit the primary schools at least once a year to discuss their children's progress. They show a 'fair level of interest' if they fall short on one of these counts, and a 'low level of interest' if they fall short on more than one.[1]

These three groups of parents differ sharply in their educational aspirations—for example, in their views on school leaving and their hopes that their children will get grammar school places. On the average, the children in these three groups are also of widely different ability and, as will be shown in the next chapter, have very different attitudes to their studies; moreover they are numerous enough for satisfactory statistical comparisons to be made among the four social classes. Although this grading gives only a crude picture of the level of the parents' interest, it has been a great aid to understanding the part played in primary school education by the support and encouragement children receive from their homes.

The parents who are most interested in their children's education come predominantly from the middle classes, and those who are least interested from the manual working classes. Within each social class, however, the parents who give their children the most encouragement in their school work also give them the best care in infancy. The manual working class parents show this more strongly[2] than the middle class parents; if they show a high level of interest in their children's school work, then their standards of care and their use of the services are also high, and they have middle class standards too in their views on the school leaving age and in their expectations of grammar school awards.

An eight-year-old child will be greatly influenced, one would imagine, by the attitude of his parents to his school work. His

[1] Table VII(a), page 155.
[2] The correlation coefficient showing the relation between the parents' interest score and the maternal care score is $+0.17$ in the middle classes and $+0.48$ in the manual working classes. (For these correlations more detailed scores running from 0–50 were used.)

own attitude to his work will be moulded by theirs and, if they are ambitious for his success, he will have the further advantage of home tuition in reading and probably other subjects.[1] Even in the early years at the primary school his test performance will show the effects of these pressures which, as he grows older and the 11+ examination approaches, are likely to increase in intensity. It is expected, then, that the parents' attitudes will have a considerable effect on the performance of children at eight years and an even greater effect on the performance of the eleven-year-olds. This is borne out by the results of this survey.[2]

At both eight and eleven years, but particularly at eleven, the highest average scores in the tests are made by the children whose parents are the most interested in their education and the lowest by those whose parents are the least interested. This is partly a social class effect stemming from the large proportion of upper middle class children among the former and of manual working class children among the latter. But the relation between the children's scores and their parents' attitudes persists within each social class. It is less marked in the middle classes than in the manual working classes, but is substantial in both and cannot be explained away in terms of social selection alone. In the upper middle class, for instance, the children of very interested parents make scores that are 3·7 points higher on the average than those made by the children of uninterested parents. In the lower manual working class they make scores that are 9·2 points higher.

The children who are encouraged in their studies by their parents do better in each type of test, in picture intelligence tests as well as in those of reading, vocabulary and arithmetic. Their advantage is, however, less in the tests which are given pictorially or in diagrammatic form. Those with very interested parents make higher scores at both eight and eleven years in the tests of school subjects than they do in the picture or non-verbal intelligence tests. At each age they may be considered

---

[1] In both the middle and manual working classes, for example, the proportion of children who were given reading lessons before they went to their primary schools is twice as high among those whose parents were later classified as showing a high level of interest, as among those showing a low level.

[2] Table VII(b), page 156.

6

as being on the average 'over-achievers', and by the same
criterion, the children of uninterested parents may be considered
'under-achievers'.[1]

The children whose parents show a high level of interest not
only make higher average scores in the tests at eight and eleven
years, but also improve the level of their performance between
these ages so that they pull ahead. After allowing for the influence
of social class, the children whose parents show a high level of
interest improve their scores by an average of 1·06 points, those
whose parents show an average interest improve by 0·29 points,
and those whose parents show little interest deteriorate by 0·18
points. The increasing advantage of the children with interested
parents cannot be explained by the changes that were made in the
types of test used at eight and eleven because it is as marked in
the reading and vocabulary tests[2] as in the combined test scores.

The children with interested parents pull ahead of the rest
whatever their initial starting ability, as is seen in the following
table:

LOWER MANUAL WORKING CLASS CHILDREN

Level of measured ability at eight	Level of Parents' Interest		
	High	Average	Low
	Change in score 8–11 years	Change in score 8–11 years	Change in score 8–11 years
40 or less	*	+2·07	+0·58
41–45	*	+0·79	−0·42
46–50	*	+2·17	−0·71
51–55	+0·60	−0·63	−0·96
56–60	+1·50	−1·65	−3·16
61 and over	−1·36	−4·00	−5·71

*Fewer than 10 children in these groups.

(+ = improved   − = deteriorated)

[1] Table VII(c), page 157.
[2] These were given in exactly the same form at eleven years as at eight.

The children who are encouraged in their work by their parents are, it seems, at an advantage both in the relatively high scores they make in the tests and in the way they improve their scores between eight and eleven years. How far is this because these children are stimulated by their parents? Could it not equally well be explained by saying that the interested parents are themselves likely to be relatively successful in life and so in a position to live in good homes and to send their children to the best schools? May not the advantages enjoyed by their children stem mainly from the better teaching they get in school and from the generally good environment in which they live? A firm answer to these questions is given in the analysis made by H. R. Simpson (see page 138) where the overlapping effects of standard of home, size of family and academic record of the school, on test performance are removed, leaving a series of adjusted average test scores which show the residual influence of parents' interest on measured ability. After these adjustments, the advantage of the children with interested parents is somewhat reduced but still considerable.

In each social class, children have a considerable advantage in the eight-year tests if their parents take an interest in their school work, and an even greater advantage at eleven. The influence of the level of the parents' interest on test performance is greater[1] than that of any of the other three factors—size of family, standard of home, and academic record of the school—which are included in this analysis, and it becomes increasingly important as the children grow older. It is among the girls especially that this effect is seen. Among the working class boys, parents' interest is only slightly more important at eleven than at eight, whereas among the middle class boys it even shows a relative decline: the test performance at eleven is then correspondingly more affected by the type of school they attend and the number of brothers and sisters they have.

As one would expect from their test scores, children do relatively well in the secondary selection examinations if their parents take much interest in their work and relatively badly if they take little interest.[2] This difference is most marked in the

[1] Greater as judged by the level of the statistical significance of its effect.
[2] Table VII(d), page 158.

manual working classes, where 40 per cent of the former and only 10 per cent of the latter go to grammar schools. The teachers, though more optimistic than the results of the 11+ examinations justify, take a similar view and consider that 59 per cent of the manual working class children are suitable for grammar schools if their parents are interested, and only 15 per cent if they are uninterested. In the middle classes also the teachers' views show a similar agreement with the results of secondary school selection and the level of the parents' interest.

The children with parents who are interested in their work do well in the secondary selection examinations and are favourably rated by their teachers largely because they are of superior measured ability at eleven. Once this factor is allowed for, they still have a slight additional advantage in the examinations; those with very interested parents get 10 per cent more places than we would expect, whereas those with uninterested parents get 7 per cent fewer. It is however the children at the borderline of the level of ability needed for grammar school entrance, who get substantially more grammar school places if their parents are interested in their work; they get 19 per cent more places than expected whereas those with uninterested parents get 14 per cent fewer.[1]

The influence of the parents on their children's chances in the secondary selection examinations is better shown when the children are grouped by the wishes their parents expressed when they were ten years old, wishes for the type of school they should go to, and how long they should stay there (see page 143).[2] This is hardly surprising, for the school interest score is an attempt to measure the level of support and encouragement which will help children of widely different ability to take an interest in their studies and use their capabilities as far as they can, whereas the wishes parents expressed for the type of school their children should go to are likely to indicate the pressures

[1] Table VII(e), page 158.

[2] Among children of measured ability between 55 and 60, i.e. those who are on the borderline for grammar school entry, those whose mothers wish them to go to grammar school and stay there till seventeen at least get 23 per cent more places than expected, those whose mothers are doubtful get 24 per cent fewer places and those who expect to go to a secondary modern school and leave before seventeen get 69 per cent fewer places than expected.

that may have been used to stimulate children of above average ability to get a valued prize.

We have seen in this chapter that children, when their parents take an interest in their work and encourage them, improve their scores in tests of school performance and mental ability between the ages of eight and eleven years and have a slight advantage in the 11 + selection examinations. On the other hand, when parents take little interest, their children lose ground in the tests and gain rather fewer places in the selection examinations than would be expected from their measured ability. The influence of the parents' attitudes on their children's behaviour in school is described in the next chapter.

CHAPTER VIII

Children's Attitudes and Behaviour

ELEVEN plus selection, as we have seen, is seldom made by tests alone, and a child who seems adequate on our tests may have a poor teacher's report, or may fail to justify himself when interviewed, and so be offered a secondary modern instead of a grammar school place. Lack of mental discipline and of application is often the key to poor work at school, and the earliest intelligence tests were designed to distinguish the children who lacked ability from the children who were lazy. As Binet and Simon put it, many years ago, 'to succeed in one's studies one must have qualities which depend especially on attention, will and character, for example, a certain docility, a regularity of habit and especially a continuity of effort.'[1] The canal boat children, for example, whose poor performance in intelligence tests appeared to be due to the cumulative effects of unstimulating home circumstances, were notably deficient in the ability to apply themselves to their work at school.[2]

When the survey children were ten years old we asked their teachers to assign them to one of five categories which varied from 'very hard-working' to 'lazy'. As is usual in such assessments, the teachers were reluctant to give an unfavourable opinion; only 17 per cent of the children, they say, work less hard than the average child, but 38 per cent work harder. Very few are prepared to say a pupil is lazy.

A high proportion of the hard workers come from the middle class families; 26 per cent of the children from the upper middle classes are said to work very hard as compared with 17 per cent of those from the lower middle class, and 11 per cent and 7 per cent from the upper and lower manual working classes. A poor assessment of work often goes with other adverse comments, as is shown in the following table.

[1] Quoted Davis, A. (1948).
[2] Neff, W. S. (1938).

	Children's Attitude to Work		
	Hard Worker	Average Worker	Poor or Lazy Worker
	%	%	%
Middle class children:			
Lacks concentration	1·2	16·8	64·8
Poor discipline	0·8	2·2	11·7
Difficulties with other children	6·1	9·5	17·1
Manual working class children:			
Lacks concentration	1·4	14·8	76·5
Poor discipline	0·3	1·8	9·4
Difficulties with other children	4·3	10·2	16·4

Children tend to work well when their parents take an interest in their school progress and to work badly when their parents are uninterested. There are, however, a substantial number who work hard even though they are given little encouragement at home.[1] The middle class children are less influenced by their parents' attitudes than the manual working class children are and tend to work hard even when their parents lack interest. This may reflect the high educational aspirations of the neighbouring middle class families from which they draw their friends or the relatively high academic level of the primary schools they attend.

The very hardworking children from each social class do well in the eleven-year tests: those from the upper middle class families make the high average score of 62·91 as compared with the low score of 48·53 made by children from the same class who are said to be poor workers; differences even larger than this are found between the hard and poor workers in the three other social classes.[2] To put this another way round, one can say

[1] Table VIII(a), page 159.
[2] Table VIII(b) and (c), pages 159 and 160.

that the clever children tend to work hard while the dull children tend to be idle. The lazy children seem to be a special group; they do better in the tests than those who are simply described as poor workers and, although there are many backward children among them, more than one would expect are of above average ability.

Do children do well in these tests, which are largely based on ability in school subjects, because they work hard, or do they seem to work hard to their teachers because they are interested and find the subjects easy? There is at least some evidence that hard work improves test performance, since in each social class the very hard-working children make higher scores at eleven than at eight, while the lazy ones and poor workers make lower scores. In other words, during these three years at primary school, the hard workers have drawn ahead of the rest. The child's attitude to work has a similar influence on performance at each level of ability and hard work leads to as great a relative improvement in test performance among the backward children as among the clever ones.

The hard workers do well, and the poor workers do badly in each type of test and there is a consistent tendency at both eight and eleven years for the hard workers to do rather better in the tests of school subjects than in the tests of non-verbal ability. To a small extent these are over-achievers and are particularly so in the arithmetic test where they make on the average a score of 60·05 as compared with a score of 57·88 in the eleven-year non-verbal ability test. In contrast the poor workers show similarly low scores in all tests and there is no evidence of a pattern of under-achievement among them.

In the previous chapter it was observed that the average test scores of children improve relatively with age if their parents take an interest in their work, and deteriorate if they do not do so. We are now able to see how much of this change may be attributed to the influence of the parents' attitudes on their children's work habits.

When the children are divided into those who 'work hard or very hard', who are 'average', or who are 'poor workers or lazy', in each group the average test score made at eleven years increases in passing from those whose parents take little interest in their work to those whose parents take much interest; but less so than when no account is taken of the children's attitude to their school work. When one looks, not at the level of test scores, but at the changes in average score between eight and eleven years, the level of interest of the parents has a negligible effect and the attitude of the children towards their work a considerable one. The hard-working children improve their scores on the average between eight and eleven years whether their parents encourage them or not, and the poor workers and lazy children deteriorate in performance whatever their parents' attitude (see the following table). It seems that parents influence the test performance of their children between the ages of eight and eleven only to the extent that they succeed or fail to encourage them to work hard.

| Level of Parents' Interest | Children's Attitude to Work | | |
| | Very Hard or Hard Workers | Average Workers | Poor Workers or Lazy |
	Change in score 8–11 years	Change in score 8–11 years	Change in score 8–11 years
High	+1·45	+1·24	—0·77
Average	+1·97	+1·57	—0·49
Low	+2·33	+0·45	—0·78

(+ = improved   — = deteriorated)

When the teachers were asked to assess the attitude of the children to their school work, we expected that the manual working class children would be particularly severely assessed in schools whose pupils were predominantly drawn from the middle classes, but this was not so, and the teachers appear to have shown remarkably little class bias in their assessments.

The children who later go to grammar schools are more likely to have worked hard during their years in the primary schools, those who go to secondary modern schools are not.[1] The private school children are rather unfavourably assessed by their teachers; there are even fewer hard workers among them than among the future secondary modern school pupils, and as many lazy ones or poor workers. This is particularly striking because they are drawn from the middle classes whose children, when they go to primary schools, are said to be among the hardest workers. In the private schools the teachers may apply different standards from those applied by the local education authority teachers.

The children who work hard or very hard get 12 per cent more grammar school places than one would expect from their test scores.[2] The poor or average workers, in contrast, get 25 per cent fewer places. At the borderline levels of ability needed for grammar school entry, the hard workers are at an even greater advantage, for example hard-working children who make scores between 55 and 60 in the eleven-year tests get 19 per cent more grammar school places than expected, whereas a similar group of children who are average or poor workers get 27 per cent fewer places. It might be thought that the very hard workers would do better than the hard workers in the secondary selection examinations, but this is not so. Comparing children of similar measured ability, the very hard workers get 11·5 per cent more grammar school places than expected and the hard workers 11.6 per cent more. It is difficult to see why the average and poor workers should do worse in the selection examinations than would be expected from their scores in the eleven-year tests. Perhaps the tests, being short, fail to take into account the powers of concentration and the habits of work of the less industrious children and so do not reveal their deficiencies to the same extent as the more searching secondary selection examinations. Or perhaps these differences simply reflect the importance given to the teachers' reports of work habits when allocating children to different types of secondary school.

Children who are not succeeding in their studies yield more

---

[1] Thirty-eight per cent of the future grammar school children were said by their primary school teachers to be very hard-working, but only 8 per cent of the future secondary modern school children were similarly assessed.

[2] Table VIII(d) and (e), pages 161 and 162.

than their share of disorderly conduct and restlessness in class; in contrast, gifted children are likely to be well-adjusted to life, and hard-working and attentive in school. The second question to be discussed in this chapter is how far the school progress of the children and their attitude to work is influenced by their emotional adjustment.

We are only able to make a crude estimate of the emotional adjustment of these children and have had to rely on the reports from their mothers amplified by less detailed reports from their teachers. In the future we hope to have a more satisfactory measure of adjustment, but the reports of Gildea and her co-workers[1] have shown that counts of symptoms such as nail-biting or thumb-sucking, given by mothers, help to identify minor or incipient behaviour disorders in their children.

A rough measure of disturbed behaviour[2] is obtained by counting the number of symptoms reported by the mothers of eleven-year-old children to the school doctors and nurses. One point was given for each of four symptoms or group of symptoms: 'bed-wetting', 'nightmares', 'abdominal pain or recurrent vomiting' and 'nail-biting, thumb-sucking and other similar habits'. The scores thus run from nought to four. These symptoms are all ones that suggest emotional maladjustment, and they are among those listed by the Underwood Committee[3] as being associated with behaviour problems in children. They may of course sometimes have a largely physical basis and, of the children who are reported to have several symptoms, some may be physically ill rather than emotionally disturbed.

There are only small differences in the number of symptoms reported for middle class and manual working class children. Bed-wetting is more common among the latter, but chiefly because nearly twice as many manual working class girls as middle class girls wet their beds. This social class difference, which is not found among the boys and has been confirmed in other studies, was noted by us at earlier ages, and persists at eleven.[4] We can as yet give no explanation for it. Allowing for the

---

[1] Gildea, M. C. L., *et al.* (1958).
[2] Douglas, J. W. B., and Mulligan, D. G. (1961).
[3] Underwood Committee (1955).
[4] Blomfield, J. M., *et al.* (1956).

social class differences in bed-wetting, the distribution of children with none, one, two, etc., symptoms is closely similar in each social class.

The children with several symptoms are likely to show other evidence of maladjustment; for example, 5·4 per cent of those with three or four reported symptoms have been to child guidance clinics as compared with only 0·1 per cent of those who are symptom-free. And the mothers who report that their children have many symptoms are worried about their behaviour in other ways. Indeed these children are surrounded by an aura of worry which may itself contribute to their difficulties. Their mothers are constantly worrying about their educational progress and their health, as well as about their behaviour. They lose an excessive amount of time from school though one cannot say yet whether this is because they are in fact more prone to minor illnesses or because their mothers are over-fussy about their health and keep them unnecessarily at home.

That we are not just recording the degree of fussiness of the mothers is evident from the independent comments of the teachers who describe many of the children with many reported symptoms as being emotionally disturbed in other ways. In open comments, which they made when the children were ten years old, the teachers described a few children as 'aggressive' and a few others as 'highly strung'. The latter include a high proportion of those who, according to their mothers when interviewed one year later, were bed-wetters or had other symptoms of disturbed behaviour. In contrast the children who were described as aggressive have no more and no fewer symptoms reported by their mothers than are reported for the rest of the children, who in the eyes of their teachers were reliable or showed no noteworthy abnormalities of behaviour.

Further independent evidence that these symptom counts have meaning is found in the test scores of these children. The eleven-year-olds who bite their nails, wet their beds, have repeated nightmares, or bouts of unexplained abdominal pain and recurrent vomiting, tend to make low scores in the tests and to deteriorate in test performance between eight and eleven years. These findings hold for each symptom taken individually and for boys and girls from each social class. They are even more pronounced when the children are grouped by the total number of symptoms they have, rather than by the individual symptoms.[1] When this is done, those with no symptoms at all make average test scores at eleven years, which are four points above those made by children with three or four symptoms. The former, moreover, improve their position in the tests by 0·22 points between eight and eleven years, whereas the latter deteriorate in performance by 1·60 points. Girls with two or more symptoms make lower average scores in the eight-year tests (49·30) than the boys do (50·08), and during the subsequent three years deteriorate in score by 0·95 points, whereas the boys with two or more symptoms deteriorate by 0·71 points. The girls are less likely to show symptoms, but when they do show them it seems that they are more affected than the boys.

The teachers find that the children with two or more symptoms are poor workers, lack concentration and have difficulties with their classmates. Twenty-two per cent of the children with no symptoms of disturbed behaviour get grammar school places as compared with 7·5 per cent of those with three or more symptoms. Part of this difference in the award of places stems from the lower measured ability of the children with many symptoms, but when this is allowed for they still fail to get the number of grammar school places for which they seem fitted by the level of their performance in the tests. The extent of handicap may be summarised by saying that the children with three or more symptoms get 22 per cent fewer places than expected after taking their measured ability into account, whereas children with two symptoms of disturbed behaviour get 10 per cent fewer places, those with one symptom 2 per cent fewer and those with no symptoms at all 5 per cent more. The children with many symptoms are most affected in their performance in the secondary selection examinations if they are at the borderline level of ability for admission to grammar schools (i.e. T scores of 55 to 60) and also come from the manual working classes; they then get 34 per cent fewer places than expected.

The conclusions of this chapter are that the attitude of children to their school work is deeply affected by the degree of encouragement their parents give them and by their own level of emotional

[1] Tables VIII(f) and (g), pages 162 and 163.

stability. The children who show few symptoms of emotional instability, and whose parents are ambitious for their academic success, have an increasing advantage during the years they are at primary school, largely because they pursue their studies with greater vigour and concentration than the less favoured children are prepared or able to do.

CHAPTER IX

Boys and Girls

AT THE secondary schools boys and girls have very different educational problems, some of which arise from the different types of career open to them, some from past prejudices not yet outgrown and some from differences in the age of onset of adolescence. Girls have for a long time found many openings in careers, such as teaching, which accept entrants at eighteen but not before and require further education but not to a university standard. Even girls going into secretarial jobs benefit by staying on at school and acquiring the general education which equips them to accept responsibility in their work, to become, for example, a personal secretary rather than a copy typist. For many girls, then, a school-leaving age of eighteen is clearly an advantage, and even for girls of moderate ambitions a grammar type of education has attractions.

For boys the position is rather different. Until recently, only a limited number of careers were open to a boy who left school at eighteen and did not proceed to a university. When the maximum age for completing apprenticeship is twenty-one and the usual age of starting is sixteen, the boy who stays on at school is at a disadvantage if he wishes to become a skilled manual worker. For this reason there is a tradition of early leaving among boys who are going into skilled manual work, whereas the majority of those who stay on at school take courses designed to prepare them for the universities or the minor professions. These different needs of boys and girls, though less marked today than in the past, are mentioned here because they affect the attitudes of both parents and children at the point of secondary selection or even earlier.[1]

Education is still seen by many not as an end in itself but as a means of getting a job. It is natural, though regrettable, that the

[1] Crowther, G. (1959).

views of parents and children should be coloured by this even in the early school years. Girls are less likely to have long-term plans for a career, and earlier adolescence and the increasing popularity of early marriage is further curtailing their initial employment years. During the last century the onset of puberty has advanced by some three and a half years, so that the majority of girls of thirteen and a half or over are today physiologically mature. In these circumstances it is not surprising that fewer girls than boys complete their grammar school courses. The relatively early age of puberty among girls also raises an important problem of secondary selection which is not encountered by boys since they mature on the average some two years later. This is discussed in the next chapter.

The aim of the 1944 Act was to give equal opportunities for secondary education to boys and girls, and the Spens report of 1938 suggested that in view of the provision of technical schools, which were primarily designed for boys, a somewhat higher grammar school provision was required for girls. The expansion of grammar school places for girls was particularly necessary at that time owing to the more generous provision already made for boys. In the present study girls are given more grammar school places than boys (20·2 per cent as compared with 18·0 per cent), but this excess is partly offset by the additional places given to boys in technical schools (4·4 per cent for girls as compared with 5·8 per cent for boys).[1] It appears then that the present distribution of grammar and technical school places to boys and girls falls a little short of the hopes of the Spens Committee, in the sense that the girls are rather more likely to go to selective secondary schools than the boys. It exceeds their hopes in another sense as 19 per cent of children go to grammar schools instead of the 15 per cent they envisaged.

There is much evidence from past studies that girls are more successful than boys in the primary schools. In reading, writing, English and spelling, the average eleven-year-old girl beats the average eleven-year-old boy. But although the girls retain their superiority in these basic subjects when they reach the secondary schools, they fall behind the boys in many others, particularly

[1] These figures include transfers to technical schools between the ages of eleven and fifteen. (See Chapter XV).

arithmetic, geography and science.[1] These observations do no necessarily imply that there are fundamental differences in the academic ability of boys and girls. It is noticeable that girls excel in subjects that are taught by women and boys in those that are taught by men. There is a danger that owing to the preponderance of men teachers of physics, chemistry and mathematics, and owing to their greater experience in teaching, these subjects will come to be thought of as 'boys' subjects' and the girls will expect, and be expected, to do badly in them. Equally the subjects taught in primary schools mainly by women may come to be thought of as 'girls' subjects' or 'women's subjects' and fail to arouse the interest of many boys on that account. We see later that the primary school teachers find the boys more idle and inattentive than the girls, and their opinion of the academic abilities of the boys is lower than our tests would justify. This suggests that they are less successful in arousing the interest of the boys than of the girls and underlines the dangers just mentioned.

In intelligence tests no clear sex differences are found; in some tests the girls are superior, in others the boys. Some have claimed that the boys are more variable in ability; that is to say there are more clever boys than clever girls as well as more backward ones. But this again seems to depend on the sort of test used. If the girls do better than the boys in the primary schools, this is more likely to be explained by their sharper interest and better relations with their teachers than by their superior 'innate' ability.

We now turn to the evidence from this survey. The tests which are mainly based on performance in school subjects show the girls as being slightly superior to the boys at both eight and eleven years, and this is so in each social class. These average figures hide considerable social class differences. In the middle classes, the boys improve their scores between eight and eleven years; they start by doing less well than the girls but have nearly caught them up by the time they are eleven. In contrast the boys from the manual working classes are as far behind the girls at eleven as they are at eight.

The picture intelligence test used at eight shows no sex

[1] Stroud, J. B., *et al.* (1942).

7

differences in ability, but it was replaced at eleven by a mixed verbal and non-verbal intelligence test which, in both its parts, favours the girls. This, accepted at its face value, suggests that the girls, as they get older, gain an intellectual advantage over the boys.[1]

The substitution of an arithmetic test at eleven years for the sentence completion test given at eight leads to further difficulties of interpretation. The girls made higher average scores than the boys in both these tests, but they had a greater advantage (1·32 points) in the sentence completion test than in the arithmetic test (where they scored 0·50 points more than the boys).

This is the over-all picture; in the middle classes, the boys surpassed the girls in the arithmetic test though they were considerably below them in the sentence completion test given when they were eight. In contrast the manual working class boys were as much below the manual working class girls in the arithmetic test as they were in sentence completion. It might be said that by substituting one type of test at eight with another type of test at eleven, we have artificially made it appear that the boys are catching up with the girls and moreover have given a special advantage to the middle class boys.

The reading and vocabulary tests provide the only valid basis for comparing the changes in achievement shown by boys and girls during the primary school years. The same tests were used at both eight and eleven and the agreement between the scores made by children at these two ages is high, equally so for each sex.[2] The girls, whatever their social class, make higher scores than the boys in the reading tests, but there is a tendency for the boys to catch up so that by the time they are eleven they have reduced their reading handicap to half of what it was at eight. The same pattern is found in each social class but is rather less marked for the manual working class boys.

At both eight and eleven years the boys have a larger vocabu-

---

[1] The boys' average score in the eight-year picture intelligence test was 50·4 3 and the girls' 50·49. The equivalent scores in the non-verbal part of the eleven-year intelligence test were 50·25 and 50·53.

[2] The correlation coefficients relating the T scores for reading at eight with the T scores for reading at eleven are +0·79 for both the boys and the girls. The corresponding coefficients for the vocabulary test are +0·70 and +0·71.

lary than the girls. In the middle classes they have an increasing advantage over the girls as they get older, but in the manual working classes they lose ground slightly.

It appears then that the boys have an advantage in some tests and the girls an advantage in others, but judging from their performance in the reading and vocabulary tests it would seem that in the middle classes, at any rate, the boys between the ages of eight and eleven have improved their performance relative to that of the girls.

Before turning to look at the results of the secondary selection examinations, we shall see how the parents view the school progress of their sons and daughters and how the teachers describe their attitude to work. The parents are rather more concerned about the progress of their daughters than of their sons. This is particularly so in the upper manual working class families where 14 per cent of the girls' parents, but only 8 per cent of the boys', show a high level of interest in their school work. The expressed aspirations of the parents for secondary education are, however, similar for both boys and girls. In their wishes for grammar school places, and in their views on the school-leaving age, they make little distinction between their sons and daughters.

The teachers tend to see the boys as less hard working, less able to concentrate and less willing to submit to discipline than the girls. These judgements are made mostly by women, and might have been different if they had been made by men. Upper middle class children appear to be better behaved at school than lower manual working class children, but the upper middle class boys are picked out as being lazier and more difficult than the upper middle class girls, just as the lower manual working class boys are picked out as being lazier and more difficult than the lower manual working class girls. There is constant criticism of the boys; for example, though the behaviour of school children is much more favourably reported on when their parents show great interest in their work, the boys still get nearly twice as much criticism as the girls.

In commenting on specific subjects the teachers say that among the ten-year-olds more boys than girls are outstandingly bad in reading, and fewer are outstandingly good. Nearly three times as many boys as girls were given extra tuition in reading. These reported differences are more marked in the manual working classes than in the middle classes; this finding, also, follows the pattern of the reading test scores.

Girls, as is mentioned on page 70, get rather more grammar school places than boys, but when allowances are made for their very slightly higher scores in the eleven-year tests, these differences are fully accounted for.[1] There are slightly more middle class girls and slightly fewer middle class boys at grammar schools than would be expected from their measured ability, though this might well have occurred by chance. It seems that grammar school places are fairly allocated between the sexes according to their measured ability; but if, as seems true in the middle classes, the measured ability of boys increases with age, what seems to be a fair distribution of places at eleven may be unfair at later ages.

Although the boys make nearly as high scores as the girls and do as well as their ability suggests in the 11+ examinations, the teachers think that many more of the girls than of the boys should be given grammar school places. Their assessment of the boys' ability is particularly unfavourable in the manual working classes where they would like to see 39 per cent more grammar school places given to the girls. In the middle classes they consider that the girls should be given only 13 per cent more places than the boys. These views are heavily influenced by the behaviour of the boys in class. The unruly boy or the boy who is idle tends to be graded by his teacher as unsuitable for a grammar school education even when, by his score in the survey tests, he should get a place. In the 11+ examinations, however, these unruly or idle children, although they do a little less well than would be expected from their test scores, do considerably better than their teachers anticipated. The women teachers, who form the majority of the primary school teachers, appear to find the boys difficult and unresponsive, as is shown in the table on page 75.

These differences in the way in which the teachers see the boys and girls are emphasised here because they suggest a lack of sympathy and understanding of the boys. This may well have undesirable effects on their behaviour in class, their progress and

[1] Table IX(a), page 164.

	Poor Worker or Lazy	Lacks Concentration	Lacks Discipline
	%	%	%
Middle class:			
Boys	11·3	17·2	3·3
Girls	6·1	8·7	1·2
Manual working class:			
Boys	23·8	27·8	3·9
Girls	14·7	17·6	1·6

their attitudes to the subjects taught in the primary schools. That this is so is suggested by the observation (see page 139) that the test scores of manual working class boys are little influenced by the type of primary school they go to, whereas the test scores of the girls are greatly influenced.

To summarise, the tests used in this survey do not clearly distinguish between the performance of boys and girls. In some tests the girls do better, in others the boys. On the average, girls do rather better than boys in each social class but the middle class boys draw nearer to the girls as they get older. The award of grammar school places to boys and girls fits closely with what would be expected from their measured ability, in spite of the fact that the teachers are more critical of the boys and consider that many fewer of them deserve grammar school places. One important point bearing on these sex differences is discussed in the next chapter, which shows the influence of sexual maturation on the test performance and 11+ examination results of girls.

CHAPTER X

Early Adolescence

MANY of the girls and a few of the boys show signs of approaching puberty when they are eleven years old. Indeed 17 per cent of the girls are then sexually mature and a further 33 per cent have early signs of puberty such as breast enlargement or the growth of pigmented pubic hair. At this age the girls are some two years ahead of the boys in their physical development. The wide range of sexual maturity among eleven-year-old children and the great difference in the level of maturity of boys and girls raises problems of secondary selection which, though generally recognised, have been insufficiently studied.

The main questions may be simply stated; do children who develop early have an advantage in the secondary selection examinations, and if so, is this justified by their later performance at school? If the early developers have only a temporary advantage, they may be keeping others out of grammar schools who would, during their later growth, catch up with or even perhaps surpass them. In this case, we should try to base selection on measures of ability that are relatively unaffected by sexual maturity and try to increase the facilities for transferring pupils from secondary modern to grammar schools, if their developing abilities make this advisable. At the present time (as is shown on page 120) such transfers rarely occur. The alternative of delaying secondary school selection until all children have passed puberty is difficult owing to the wide spread of the age of reaching full maturity.

The following observations are limited to the girls because a measurable sign of sexual maturity is provided by the onset of menstruation, whereas the sexual development of the boys can only be described in anatomical terms, which do not give a precise date for the beginning of puberty. It might have been better to use some other measure of maturity such as bone-age or the age of maximum physical growth, for this would have given a physiologically valid criterion of the level of maturity of the boys as well as of the girls. This was, however, impracticable in the setting of this inquiry; frequently repeated bodily measurements could not be reasonably asked for, nor could radiographic plates. This is not necessarily a loss, for these refined criteria of development may miss out a description of gross bodily changes that are of greater importance than an exact determination of physiological maturity, when it comes to observing the effects of puberty on mental and emotional development.

Girls today reach sexual maturity earlier than they did in the past. In Norway, which has the most complete records of any country, the average age at which girls had their first period was seventeen one hundred and fifty years ago as compared with thirteen today.[1] During these years there has been a progressive decline in the average age of puberty which has advanced by approximately four months every ten years. British records are less complete and far less extensive than the Norwegian ones, though they show the same trend. There must come a lower limit to this advancement of puberty though there is no sign that it is yet in sight. The most recent information shows that the trend has been well maintained in recent years, and that London school girls in 1959 started their periods when they were, on the average, three months younger than would have been expected from the records of five years back.[2]

There is no similar historical information about the sexual development of boys. It is doubtful whether there can have been such a profound change as has been recorded for the girls. If so, boys living one hundred and fifty years ago would have been on the average nineteen years old before they were sexually mature, and contemporary writings do not suggest that this was so. On the other hand London school boys in recent years have also shown an advancement of puberty. Half of the boys had broken voices at thirteen years ten months in 1959 as compared with half at fourteen years two months in 1954.[2]

It is beyond the range of this study to discuss the many important problems raised by the trend towards early puberty; the following analysis is limited to a description of the type of girls

[1] Tanner, J. M. (1961).
[2] London County Council (1961).

whose sexual development is early or delayed, their performance in the survey tests, and in the secondary selection examinations.

The information on sexual maturity was given by the school doctors who examined the girls when they were eleven and fifteen years old, and reported on their physical development and when their periods had started. As already mentioned, 17 per cent of eleven-year-old girls were by these criteria sexually mature. This is a small proportion and it is more satisfactory[1] to divide them according to the information obtained at fifteen which shows that 39 per cent started their periods before the age of twelve years ten months; 33 per cent between twelve years ten months and thirteen years nine months, and 28 per cent[2] later than this. The first group are referred to as the 'early-developers', and the last group as the 'late-developers'.

It is generally considered that the continuing trend towards early puberty is a reflection of the improving nutrition of the poorer families. There is little doubt that in the past the children of manual workers were on the average slower in reaching puberty than the children of the well-to-do. In the last century there was a two-year gap in this respect between Italian girls from the professional and labouring classes and a similar social class difference was reported from Denmark as recently as thirty-five years ago. The relation between social class and the rate of sexual development does not appear to have been studied in Britain in recent years, and the present survey gives the most complete figures yet available. They are surprising, for the manual working class girls, instead of reaching puberty later than the middle class girls, if anything precede them, and the upper middle class girls are on the average the latest developers.[3] A more detailed study of these families fails to show any positive association between poor living conditions and late puberty; in the middle classes it is the *late* developers who tend to come from the better homes, from those which were least crowded and best equipped and which possessed a television set, telephone or

---

[1] Satisfactory in the statistical sense. Similar pictures are given whether the children are classified by the fifteen- or by the eleven-year information.

[2] This figure includes those who had not started their periods at fifteen.

[3] Table X(a), page 165.

car. There is no such consistent pattern in the manual working classes; in some respects the late developers are slightly better off, in other respects they are worse off.

The girls are classified by information given when they were fifteen and it might be argued that social class differences in the date of onset of menstruation have been obscured by errors of memory. However, this criticism cannot be levelled against the doctors' descriptions of breast development and the growth of axillary and pubic hair which also suggest that the rate of sexual development is similar in each social class. Why should there be no social class differences in sexual maturation when there are considerable ones in growth? This question might be answered if we had records to show how the social classes differed in physical growth and sexual development earlier in this century. But these do not exist and we cannot say whether the trend towards earlier puberty has affected all social classes equally or been more evident in some than in others. (This is an example of the widespread lack of information on the simple facts of human growth which, if the need had been recognised, the school medical service could have supplied.)

It has been noted elsewhere that children from small families mature earlier sexually than those from large. This was generally interpreted as showing the effects of nutrition since the money spent per head on food declines as families get larger. This relationship between family size and sexual development is also found in the present study. In particular only children reach puberty early, 53 per cent of them starting their periods before they are twelve years ten months old as compared with 39 per cent of those who have one brother or sister and 34 per cent of those who have four or more brothers or sisters.[1] This is not quite the pattern to be expected if nutrition is the underlying cause of the differences. It is difficult to believe that the nutritional level of only children is far enough above that of children in families of two, to explain their substantially earlier sexual development. This might be so in the manual working classes, but hardly in the middle classes where the difference between children from one- and two-child families is just as great. Equally, if nutrition is the cause, it is difficult to see why there

[1] Table X(b), page 165.

should be so little difference between the rate of sexual development of children with one brother or sister and those with three or more, since it is particularly in these large families that poverty is found and that spending on food is reduced.

The school doctors, after the medical examinations, were asked to give their assessments of the children's physical development and mental alertness. It was to be expected that they should pick out the early developers as being physically superior to the rest of the children at eleven years of age, but they also did so at six, though with less confidence. These by-eye assessments of physique are supported by the measurements they took during the examinations, which show that, even before they reach puberty, the girls who are going to develop early are slightly taller than those who are going to develop late, though less so than they are at eleven. The doctors also describe these girls as more alert than the late developers and they favour them in this respect as much at six years of age as at eleven.

The teachers say that the girls who develop early are superior in many ways to the rest. They work harder in school, have better powers of concentration, are more amenable to discipline, more reliable, and less likely to be shy or aggressive. More of them are outstandingly good at academic subjects, and their teachers think that their chances of getting grammar school places are higher. All these favourable comments from the doctors and the teachers apply as much to the manual working as to the middle class children.

Adolescence is often thought of as a period of emotional stress and unbalanced behaviour, but there is no evidence of this in the reports of the mothers or teachers. The early developers are not picked out as showing more behaviour problems at home or in school than the late developers and their mothers are no more worried about them.

There is a sudden spurt in physical growth just before the onset of puberty and, by analogy, it has been suggested that there is a spurt in mental growth coinciding with this. There is little to support this view however. Children who, owing to glandular disturbances become sexually mature at an unusually early age, are also precocious in height and weight, but their mental ability is not above that of the other children of their age. The few studies which follow the mental development of children from infancy to adolescence fail to show an acceleration in the growth of mental ability as puberty approaches. The children who develop early are superior in ability, but their superiority is as marked in early childhood as when they reach maturity.

This is also found in the present inquiry. The survey children who develop early score on the average two points more than the late developers in the tests of mental ability and school achievement, and the following table shows that their advantage was just as great when they were eight years old, that is to say well before they showed any sign of puberty, as at eleven.

	Age at First Period		
	Before 12 yrs 10 mths	12 yrs 10 mths to 13 yrs 9 mths	13 yrs 10 mths or later
Average test scores at:			
11 years	51·47	50·38	49·26
8 years	51·43	50·47	49·23

It used to be thought that the higher measured ability of early developers could be largely explained by the greater proportion of middle class children among them. But today this is certainly not the explanation since there are no social class differences in the ages at which these children reach puberty. The superior ability of those who develop early is, moreover, evident in each social class to approximately the same extent.

Taken as a group the early developers, as would be expected from their performance in the eleven-year tests, and from their teachers' favourable comments, are more likely than the late developers to get grammar school places. There is no more to it than this, for at each level of measured ability the girls who are immature are just as likely to go to grammar schools as those who are mature. The qualities of reliability and concentration, of alertness and superior physical development, which the teachers and school doctors attribute to the early developers, do not give them an additional advantage in the selection examinations apart from that inherent in their superior performance in the eleven-year tests.

Although the girls who mature early have superior measured ability at eleven years, there is no certainty that they retain this advantage in later school life. Several studies on small groups of girls[1] suggest that from the age of seventeen onwards the late developers catch up and that by the time of entry to the University they are academically more successful than the early developers. It may be that the latter remain superior in ability but are withdrawn from competition in the higher forms and the Universities through early marriage. It is important to know what is happening. If the early developers retain their superiority in performance throughout their school life there is no reason to allow for maturity when selecting for secondary schools, but if they lose their initial advantage and the late developers catch up, we are selecting inefficiently and should do something about it. Moreover, if the early developers are removed through marriage from the sixth forms and from the Universities, we may be losing some of our most able women from academic life, and this is something we should try to prevent.

Using the latest information it seems that the early developers in this study are as likely to stay on at school after fifteen as the late, and in the manual working classes tend to stay on longer. Looking ahead the teachers expect that a higher proportion of the early developers will stay at school till they are seventeen or older; this forecast may not be fulfilled, but it suggests at least that this group of children are still at fifteen years of age the most promising of their pupils.

What has been said in this chapter does not prove that the superior ability of the early developers stems from their greater physical maturity. It is more likely that the explanation lies in the high proportion of these girls who come from small families, and who are only children. It is most suggestive that at eleven years the measured ability of only children bears no relation to their stage of sexual development, those who mature early and those who mature late score on the average exactly the same ($53 \cdot 03$),

[1] Abernethy, E. M. (1936).

and the intermediate group scores 54·74. In larger families, taken individually by size, the early developers make scores that are on the average a little higher than those made by the late developers, though their superiority is less marked than for the sample of children taken as a whole, i.e., when no allowances are made for differences in family size. In these larger families there are additional complications such as the individual's position in the family and the spacing between births. It is the case of the only child that is crucial. By showing that the level of measured ability of this group is unrelated to their sexual development, a strong case has been made for discarding the view that this factor need be taken into account in secondary selection or that, as some have suggested, this relationship explains the recorded increases in the measured intelligence of girls in recent years.

The findings of this chapter, then, may be summarised by saying that the girls who reach puberty early are superior in behaviour and measured ability. These advantages, however, are not to be attributed to their greater physical maturity, but to the fact that a large proportion of them are only children or come from small families. The question of family size is discussed in the following chapters.

CHAPTER XI

Position in Family

THE experiences of a child, inside the home and out of it, are influenced to a considerable extent by his position in the family, by whether for example he is an only child or the eldest or youngest one. First-born children, from their earliest years, are subjected to a great deal of stimulation by adults, which their later-born brothers and sisters may miss. They are closer to their parents — on the other hand they miss the stimulus of having older children to play with. The first-born child may suffer from the inexperience of his parents, and his younger brothers and sisters may reap the benefit of the lessons learnt at his expense. At school, the first-born child is often absent in the early years, owing to childish infections which he passes on to the other members of his family, so that when they come to school in their turn they have acquired immunity and lose less schooling. A less direct influence on first-born children will come from the fact that, in many families, they have the new clothes and the new toys and pass them on to their younger brothers and sisters.

The youngest child might be expected to enjoy considerable advantages in education. In poor families, the extra money brought into the home by elder brothers and sisters who are out at work, might allow the parents to keep him at school after fifteen. It might also encourage them to send him to a grammar school because with the help of the older children they can afford to buy the necessary uniform, and forego his later earnings. The youngest children, moreover, when provisions for education are expanding, will have better opportunities than their elder brothers and sisters for going to grammar schools and for proceeding to the Universities or other forms of higher education.

Later-born children learn to talk earlier than first-born and some workers have claimed—though, as we shall see, this is not supported by the results of the present study—that within a given size of family measured intelligence increases with the birth rank of the child up to the eighth birth at least.[1] The

[1] Steckel, M. L. (1930).   Thurstone, L. L., and Jenkins, R. L. (1931).

84

sex of the children too is said to be of importance; girls with elder brothers do better than those with elder sisters.[1] Perhaps competition with a boy makes a younger sister more alert; or perhaps she is spurred on by jealousy of the extra attention that parents so often give their sons.

There is a difficulty in interpreting these comparisons of the mental ability of brothers and sisters. In recent years there has been a steady rise in the level of test performance of children and for this reason alone the younger children are likely to do better today in these tests than their elder brothers and sisters did in the past. That this may explain the apparent rise in measured ability with increasing birth rank within families is suggested by the results of the Scottish Mental Survey of 1947.[2] In this survey all the children were of the same age, eleven years, and comparisons between elder and younger children from different families showed no consistent relationship between birth rank and test score in any size of family or in either sex. In a further study in which the younger brothers and sisters of some of the Scottish survey children were tested, no evidence was found of any relation between I.Q. and order of birth.[3]

In later life it seems that the eldest child stands out as superior in achievement. Galton, for example,[4] observed that distinguished English men of science were more often eldest or only sons than younger sons. He qualified this by saying that eldest sons were 'more likely to become possessors of independent means and therefore able to follow the pursuits that have most attraction to their tastes; they are treated more as companions by their parents and have earlier responsibility both of which would develop independence of character; probably also the first-born of families not well-to-do in the world would generally have more attention in his infancy, more breathing space and better nourishment than his younger brothers and sisters in their several turns'.

More recent studies in America and Italy have confirmed Galton's observations but not resolved his criticisms. Scientists

[1] Koch, H. L. (1954).
[2] Scottish Council (1949).
[3] Maxwell, J., (1961).
[4] Galton, F. (1874).

and university professors are drawn selectively from the eldest and, to a lesser extent, from the youngest sons; the eldest sons too get more than their fair share of print in the *Dictionary of National Biography*.

The best educated parents have had in the past the smallest families and the worst educated have had the largest. A group of eldest children or for that matter of youngest children chosen today will be drawn from the more favoured families and for this reason alone they are likely to do outstandingly well at school and then proceed to a university. This does not explain Galton's observations of ninety years ago, for in those days the size of families bore little relation to the social class or education of the parents. Only in the highest ranks of society were efforts at family planning widespread and effective. Today, however, family size cannot be left out of any discussion of the relation between birth rank and achievement.

By the time they were eleven years old the majority of the survey children had as many brothers and sisters as they were ever likely to have. A few children have been born in these families since then and so a few of those called here 'the youngest' have been displaced from this position by a new baby. This does not in any way detract from the following observations, for the children who were later displaced were in fact the youngest during the period of their lives with which we are now concerned.

In this survey, as in the 1947 Scottish study, comparisons can only be made between children drawn from different families. This has the advantage that one is comparing children of the same age, who have had the same sort of schooling and the same sort of experience with mental tests. It has the disadvantage that the parents of later-born children are on the average older than the parents of first-born children and may have different educational aspirations. This disadvantage is reduced if only one, two and three child families are considered, and this is in any case advisable as there are relatively few survey children from larger families.

The first aim of this chapter is to describe, within the limits of this survey, the ways in which the upbringing and home circumstances of children differ with their birth rank; the second is to show how far, if at all, these differences influence the performance of the children in tests and in the secondary selection examinations. We are concerned with two main types of comparison, first the only children contrasted with the first-born children who have one or two brothers or sisters, and second, the first-born children contrasted with the later-born children within families of two or three.

In no social class does the only child enjoy a substantial advantage over the first-born child with one brother or sister. The homes of only children tend to be better equipped and maintained, also less crowded; their mothers are more favourably assessed by the health visitors for standards of child care, and by the teachers for the interest they take in their school progress; but these are marginal differences.

In the whole sample, the only children do very slightly better than the elder children in the tests of mental ability and school achievement, but the small differences recorded might well have occurred by chance and are not consistent between the social classes.[1] When it comes to the 11+ examinations, the only children do slightly less well than expected and in each social class get fewer grammar school places in relation to their measured ability than the elder children. They are, as is seen in the following table, at a disadvantage when their measured ability is between 55 and 60, that is to say at the borderline level for admission to grammar schools. Does lack of competition at home lead to lack of competitiveness at school?

Test Score at eleven years	Middle Class		Manual Working Class	
	Only Child at Grammar School	Eldest of 2 or 3 at Grammar School	Only Child at Grammar School	Eldest of 2 or 3 at Grammar School
	%	%	%	%
49–54	1·4	17·4	7·8	5·7
55–57	22·5	40·4	19·0	33·6
58–60	51·3	65·0	48·8	57·9
61 and over	88·1	83·1	87·5	78·9

[1] Table XI(a) and (b), pages 166 and 167.

8

The second comparison is between first- and later-born children in families of two or three. The standard of care given to first-born infants does not seem in general to be either better or worse than that given to the later-born of the same sized family. The health visitors, however, report that middle class women with three children give less good care to their first than to their later children. Deficiencies are likely to be more easily noticed in homes where high standards are expected, and the health visitors may single out these mothers just because their children are less smartly dressed and less clean than the other middle class children living around them. The middle class mother, when a new baby arrives, may find it difficult to cope with her older child and home, and so fall obviously though temporarily below the high standards expected of her.

That these early criticisms do not signify real lack of interest or failure of care is suggested by the high ambitions these same middle class mothers have for their eldest children's progress at school. They visit the schools more often and are said by the teachers to show more interest in the work of their eldest children than of their second or youngest, and they are more anxious for their eldest to go to grammar school and stay there after sixteen.

Mothers are more worried about their first- than about their later-born children. These excessive worries are not justified by our records. First-born children, it is true, are more often prematurely born and in the first year at school they lose rather more time through illness than the other children. But their record of few hospital admissions and illnesses in early life shows them as having an advantage over their younger brothers and sisters. Although the mothers seem to be excessively worried about the behaviour of their eldest children, they do not report an excess of disturbed behaviour symptoms among them; it is the last- rather than the first-born children who are more likely to wet their beds, have nightmares, pick their noses or suck their thumbs. The teachers also do not single out the first-born children for criticism. These children work as hard in class as the later-born and as a group are not conspicuous for any lack of concentration or discipline. It is only in their relations with other children that both teachers and mothers report that the elder

children have difficulties and these, as is shown in the following
table, are as marked for the middle as for the manual working
class children, and for the elder in two-child families as for the
eldest in three.

	Elder of Two	Younger of Two	Eldest of Three	Youngest of Three
	% with difficulties	% with difficulties	% with difficulties	% with difficulties
Middle classes	9·0	6·9	12·5	7·0
Manual working classes	11·3	8·7	9·0	1·9

The average test scores made by first- and later-born children
show no consistent differences in either two- or three-child
families, and there is certainly no evidence from this study that
within families the level of measured ability increases with birth
rank.[1] It does seem, however, that between eight and eleven
years the first-born children improve their test scores in relation
to their younger brothers and sisters. For example, in the upper
manual working class families of three children, during this period
the eldest improve by 0·80 points of test score and the last-born
deteriorate by 0·31 points; similar changes are found in two-child
families and this pattern is repeated in the middle classes.

The first-born children in families of two or three do better
in the secondary selection examinations than would be expected
from their measured ability at eleven and the later-born do worse.
This is found, to a greater extent, as the following table shows, in
the manual working classes. Among the clever children the
chances of going to a grammar school are as good for the eldest
as for the youngest but at the borderline of ability it is the eldest
who have an advantage. There is nothing to support the view so
often propounded that the youngest child in a manual working
class family is particularly likely to be sent to a grammar school.

[1] Table XI(b), page 167.

Test score at eleven years	Middle Class		Manual Working Class	
	Two- and Three-Child Families		Two- and Three-Child Families	
	Eldest	Youngest	Eldest	Youngest
	% at Grammar School	% at Grammar School	% at Grammar School	% at Grammar School
49–54	17·4	5·9	5·7	4·6
55–57	40·4	40·2	33·6	16·7
58–60	65·0	53·1	57·9	38·8
61 and over	83·1	92·2	78·9	78·2

The findings of this chapter are largely negative. It seems, however, that the eldest children, though they do not show any marked superiority in the tests, receive a stimulus which the younger children lack and which spurs them on to do well in the secondary selection examinations. And it seems that this stimulus is the presence of a younger child in the family, rather than the fact of being the first-born, since the only children, in contrast to the first-born in larger families, get the number of grammar school places that would be expected from their eleven-year test scores, and no more. Lastly, there is no evidence at all to support the view that in working class families the youngest child has a better chance of going to a grammar school.

CHAPTER XII

Completed Family Size

IT HAS frequently been observed that children from large families make lower scores in intelligence tests than children from small families, and are less successful at school. Clever children of course are found in large families as well as in small, but the average level of measured ability declines with each increase in completed family size. This decline is often explained by saying that intelligent couples restrict the number of their children, whereas less intelligent couples often fail to do so. As the intelligence of children tends to resemble that of their parents, it follows that on the whole those from small families will be mentally better endowed than those from large. If the duller members of the community are producing more children than the clever ones, it would seem that each generation is replacing itself by another of lower ability; if so, as Pearson put it, the future will be marked by 'a dearth of great ability and a surfeit of dullness'.[1] This gloomy view implies that in the past, before the knowledge and practice of birth control was widespread, there was no difference, or certainly less difference, between the ability of children from large and small families than there is today. There is no direct evidence that this was ever so, for by the time efficient mental tests were developed the present pattern of family limitation was well established. Galton's observations[2] on the pre-eminence of only and eldest sons among British scientists may, however, be interpreted as showing that, at a time when there were no effective restrictions on fertility, the children from small families, even if they were not more intelligent than children from larger ones, made more effective use of their talents.

The few direct comparisons that have been made between the measured intelligence of children from different generations suggest that the level of national intelligence is increasing rather than declining. For example, the American Army recruits of

[1] Quoted in Hsiao, H. H. (1931).
[2] Galton, F. (1874).

World War II made nigher scores than the recruits of World War I, when given the same intelligence test.

A more impressive example which is not open to any criticism of biased sampling, comes from the Scottish Mental Survey[1] in which the measured intelligence of all eleven-year-old Scottish children in 1932 was compared with that of all eleven-year-olds in 1947. During these fifteen years the average level of performance improved, especially that of the girls. In spite of this the decline in average test score in passing from small families to large was as marked in 1947, as it had been in 1932. This paradox has been interpreted in a number of ways. Perhaps the eleven-year-olds in 1947 had a wider experience of taking intelligence tests and this masked a real decline in ability. Or perhaps in the past too little weight has been given to the influence on mental growth of the deficiencies that so often go with large families, especially when the children are closely spaced; deficiencies such as cramped living space, low standards of care in infancy and childhood or lack of high educational aspirations and incentives at later ages.

The information collected in the present survey allows us to look more closely at the extent to which children from large families suffer from these deficiencies and at how their test scores and school performance are affected. First of all, however, it is desirable to see whether the relationship between family size and mental ability which has been shown in other studies holds for this one too. The answer is that it does. The test scores of these eleven-year-olds decline as families get larger, so that the children with five brothers or sisters make scores that are on the average 6·9 points of T score below that of only children. As each child is added to the family, so the average test score drops by a little more than that observed in the Scottish Mental Survey.[2]

It seems that in the ten years between 1947 and the present study, the relation between the mental ability of eleven-year-olds and the size of family they come from has remained substantially

---

[1] Scottish Council (1949).

[2] i.e. 0·15 standard deviation units decrease in average score per unit increase in family size, as compared with the 0·13 units decrease recorded by the Scottish Survey. (In the present study the standard deviation of the eleven year T scores is 8·92.)

unchanged. Examination of the individual test scores shows that the children from large families are at both eight and eleven years a little more handicapped in reading, arithmetic and the understanding of words, than in tests of non-verbal intelligence.

Looking back to their performance in the eight-year tests, the children from large families are seen to be nearly as much handicapped then as they are at eleven, and the children from small families nearly as much advanced. It would seem, then, that if the explanation for the poor performance of children in large families lies in deficiencies of care or in bad home conditions, these must exert their main effects before the children are eight years old.[1]

The relation between intelligence and family size, one might suspect, would be least marked at the extreme ends of the social scale. At the top, all married couples know about birth control methods and are sufficiently intelligent to use them successfully if they wish to, so that large families are a matter of preference rather than a result of ignorance or inefficiency. At the bottom, the knowledge and practice of birth control may be so defective, and failures to prevent unwanted conceptions so common at each level of intelligence, that the relation between family size and intelligence is diminished.

The middle class children do indeed show a less dramatic fall in average test score in passing from those in small families to those in large. It is not until families of four or more children are reached that there is a substantial fall in score and even beyond this size the fall is gradual up to families of eight or more. There is, however, no group of families in the middle classes where the influence of family size on the level of test score is absent; indeed, children from really large families (of six or more) are as much at a disadvantage if their fathers are in the professions, as if they follow some other middle class employment.[2]

Among the lower manual workers the relation between family size and ability is a little less marked than in the upper manual workers, but still considerable. When the class boundary is more finely drawn to include only the families of men who in 1957 were unskilled labourers, then there is virtually no deterioration in the average test scores as family size increases; it is only

[1] Tables XII(*a*) and (*b*), pages 168 and 169.
[2] See Table on next page.

AVERAGE TEST SCORES OF SURVEY CHILDREN AT ELEVEN YEARS

| | Number of Children in Family | | | | | |
	1	2	3	4	5	6 or more
Children of men in the professions	60·93	59·66	59·34	58·77	55·50	51·25
All upper middle class children	59·87	57·31	55·80	56·49	55·65	54·20

among children with five or more brothers and sisters (and there are few of them) that there is a substantial fall in average performance. It would, however, be a mistake to interpret this finding as showing that family size has no influence on the intelligence of children in the poorest class; selective factors are at work.

As already noted, there has been a great deal of movement over the years in and out of the ranks of unskilled labour, and if one takes the families of men who were in unskilled work in 1946 instead of those in 1957, a different pattern is found. As is shown in the following table, the children from these families who have many brothers and sisters are as much at a disadvantage in the tests as are children from large families in any other social class. The probable explanation is that the more intelligent labourers tend to move out of unskilled and into semi-skilled and skilled manual occupations and are more likely to be able to do so if their families are small than if they are large. On the other hand, the ranks of unskilled labour have been added to by semi-skilled manual workers with large families who might have remained as semi-skilled if their home commitments had been less heavy. The children from these families will on the average do better in the tests than the children of the residual unskilled workers. Accordingly the mean test scores of the children from the larger families will be raised.

There is a wide range of parental ages in this study; some parents were married in the 1920s, others only in 1945. It might be thought that the fertility of the early marriages would follow the pattern of past times when large families were more uniformly

Average Test Scores of Survey Children at Eleven

Unskilled labourers	Number of Children in Family					
	1	2	3	4	5	6 or more
1957	47·50	46·82	47·31	46·77	46·60	43·92
1946	49·04	49·02	46·02	46·03	44·22	40·69

distributed throughout the population than they are today, and that the relation between family size and intelligence would be less marked among them than among the more recently married couples. The results of the Scottish Mental Survey supported this hypothesis; there was a tendency for the scores of children of older mothers to become increasingly superior to those of children of younger mothers as family size increases.[1]

This observation is not confirmed in the present study; on the contrary it is the children of the youngest parents who show the least deterioration in measured ability as family size increases.[2] It would be foolhardy in the face of the findings of the Scottish Survey and of the small size of the differences we observed to say categorically that the influence of family size on test performance is less for the more recently married. This view would, however, be consistent with the results of recent studies in the United States and elsewhere, which show that it is the youngest parents who use birth control the most effectively both for planning the size of their families and the spacing of their children.

The number of grammar school places given to children in large families falls a little below that expected from their scores in the eleven-year tests. This deficiency is only found with children in families of four or more, who get 14 per cent fewer grammar school places than expected, and then it is largely the children with test scores at the borderline of grammar school acceptance who suffer. The brighter children, who have large numbers of brothers and sisters, get very nearly as many places,

[1] Maxwell, J. (1953).
[2] Table XII(c), page 170.

in relation to their ability, as the children from small families.[1]

The main question to be considered in this chapter is how much of the poor performance of the children from large families stems from deficiencies of care and from unsatisfactory home circumstances. The impact of family size is greater on the manual working than on the middle class children, whether it is judged by the standards of care and school interest,[2] or level of housing or education. In the middle classes it is only the child from a large family of four or more who is handicapped, whereas in the manual working classes the children are progressively handicapped with every increase in family size. In infancy, when their mothers are coping with the needs of several young children, the standards of medical and bodily care given to the children from large manual working class families tend to be poor. Many are taken irregularly to the child welfare centres and diphtheria immunisation is often overlooked. The health visitors describe these mothers as poor managers, giving their children and homes inferior care. Perhaps the health visitors are over-critical of dirt and slovenliness in these families and may therefore miss important aspects of good mothering; it may be also that the lack of contact of these children with their busy mothers is compensated for by the companionship of their brothers and sisters and the give and take of life in a large family. These, however, are aspects we were unable to study owing to the large number and wide dispersion of the children.

Large families are often found in the least desirable dwellings. The buildings are old and shabby; they have often no running hot water and have bathrooms and kitchens that are shared with other families. As more children arrive, their parents economise by cutting down on the rent, and they suffer for doing so in overcrowding and discomfort; thus the mothers who have the greatest domestic problems also have the worst amenities. Living space is restricted, beds are likely to be shared with brothers or sisters, sometimes with adults, and a quiet room that can be set aside for homework is seldom to be found. Economy does not stop with reducing the rent; nutritional surveys show that the amount spent per head on food falls as families grow larger and

[1] Table XII(d), page 170.
[2] Table XII(e), page 171.

that it is not only the luxuries that are cut out. The children from large families are at a disadvantage in these respects in each social class, but most of all when their parents come from the lower manual working class.

Once they start school the children from large families appear to get less encouragement from their parents than the rest of the children. Here again it is particularly the manual working class children who suffer. This may be a fault of our assessment of interest which is largely based on the teachers' contacts with the parents. Even an educationally ambitious mother may fail to visit the school, if she is tied by the needs of her younger children. But there is other evidence to suggest that mothers with many children to look after are in fact less interested; they expect their children to leave school at an early age and they are less likely to want them to get grammar school places. While all the social classes show a similar pattern, the expressed aspirations of middle class parents remain high until there are four or more children, whereas those of the manual working class parents decline with every increase in family size.

Other deficiences, which will be described in subsequent chapters, should be briefly mentioned here. The academically successful schools[1] take fewer pupils from large families than would be expected and within the schools these children stand less chance of being placed in the top stream, even when they are competing with other children of the same level of measured ability. To the deficiencies of their homes, it seems, must be added deficiencies at school. That they go to the academically less successful schools may reflect the lack of interest of their parents; that they are put in the lower streams may reflect their teachers' poor assessment of personal qualities other than measured ability. Certainly the teachers are rather more likely to pick them out as being poor workers, as lacking powers of concentration, and as being difficult to discipline. Their criticisms, however, were made at the end of the primary school period and may be a result, rather than a cause, of their allocation to low streams.

It has already been observed that the influence of family size on the level of test score is less marked on the average in the

[1] See page 104.

middle than in the manual working classes; this is indeed what
would be expected if it were in part or whole explained by
deficiencies of care and teaching. When account is taken of the
major deficiencies affecting children from large families, their
handicaps in the tests of ability and school achievement are much
reduced, and this holds for manual working class as well as
middle class children. Among the children of very interested
parents, for example, or among the children attending the
academically most successful schools, those from large families
do nearly as well in the tests as those from small. When the
combined effects of the overlapping influences of poor housing,
lack of parents' interest and poor schooling are allowed for (see
page 133), the children from large families are still at a disadvantage as compared with those from small, but less so than
before these allowances were made. The results of these adjustments are shown in the following table:

| | Boys | | Girls | |
| | Average test scores at eleven | | Average test scores at eleven | |
	Unadjusted*	Adjusted*	Unadjusted	Adjusted
Middle Class:				
1 or 2 child families	57·27	56·90	56·64	56·28
4 child or larger families	52·52	53·85	54·45	55·96
Difference in score	4·75	3·05	2·19	0·32
Manual Working Class:				
1 or 2 child families	50·00	49·22	50·98	50·07
4 child or larger families	45·53	46·46	46·07	47·27
Difference in score	4·47	2·76	4·91	2·80

* See page 133.

The great reduction for middle class girls should be noted; at neither eight nor eleven years does family size exert a statistically significant influence on their performance in the tests, whereas it has a considerable influence on the performance of middle class boys. In the eleven-year tests, for example, the middle class girls in small families of one or two children score on the average 56·28 (after adjustment) and the girls in families of four or more 55·96. For the middle class boys the equivalent figures are 56·90 and 53·85, a much wider range.

One can hardly suggest in the light of these figures that, in the middle classes at any rate, the parents who have large families are the duller ones and so have duller children. This certainly does not hold for the middle class girls, and if it doesn't hold for them how can one suggest that it holds for the boys?

It was mentioned earlier in this chapter that there was no evidence that children from large families deteriorated in their test performance between eight and eleven years. H. R. Simpson's analysis confirms this view and shows that the influence of family size on the level of test score has exerted its full effect by eight years.[1]

In conclusion, it seems that the association of family size with the level of measured intelligence is approximately as great today as it was ten years ago. Children in large families suffer more deficiencies of care in infancy and childhood and in their homes. But as the effects of family size on test performance are just as great at eight years as at eleven, it seems that these deficiencies, if they do account for part of the poor performance of these children, take their effect in early life. When allowance is made statistically for these environmental deficiencies, the influence of family size is reduced but still present. There is, however, a circularity in the attempt to assess the effect of adverse environmental circumstances by this kind of analysis, because these adverse circumstances may only be a by-product of the failure of the parents to provide for their children's needs, a failure which may in its turn stem from their low mental ability. This reasoning, however, fails to explain why the influence of family size on measured ability is less for the first- than for the later-born middle class children, and why, after allowing for the effect of

[1] Appendix II, Table B, page 137.

environment, it is very small for middle class girls but considerable for middle class boys. Other evidence that the traditional
'hereditary' explanation is not all-sufficient lies in our inability
to find a social level above which family size has no influence on
intelligence. It is indeed difficult to believe that large families in
the professional classes owe their existence to inefficiency or
ignorance of family planning—it seems more likely that the
considerable differences observed at this social level in the average
measured ability of children from small and large families are of
environmental origin. This is to be interpreted in its broadest
sense to include deficiencies of parental care as well as of the
material background of the home.

CHAPTER XIII

The Primary Schools

SO FAR the educational progress of these children has been set against the background of their families and homes; we now have to consider the influence of their schools. It should be said at once that although a great deal is known about the primary schools the children went to, we cannot make a direct assessment of the quality of teaching. As we were working through 144 local education authorities and as the children were scattered in 3,060 different primary schools there was no opportunity to assess the skill of the teachers in a uniform and reliable way. We have, therefore, inferred the quality of teaching from the past success of these schools in sending their pupils to grammar schools—a method which is clearly open to criticism. In spite of this the following observations concerning the influence of the primary schools on educational progress are sufficiently interesting and consistent to bear detailed discussion.

At the time when these children took the eleven-year tests of mental ability and school achievement, their headmasters or headmistresses were asked to give a detailed description of each school. They described the buildings in terms of their age, the extent of modernisation, the type of site and the amenities provided for staff and pupils. They gave the number of staff and the number of pupils and estimated the proportion of the latter who had fathers in the professions, in agriculture or in unskilled manual work; they also gave various other details including information about special conditions of entry.[1]

Their answers show a familiar picture of crowded class rooms and of schools which are grossly lacking in amenities. Forty-five per cent of the children are taught in classes of 40 or more. Primary schools built in the nineteenth century accommodate 48 per cent of the children and of these old schools nearly half

[1] Other details asked for were: whether maintained or independent, denominational or undenominational, primary schools only or junior departments of secondary schools.

have not been modernised in any way since the war. Amenities such as electric light, hot water, efficient sanitation, an adequate playground, a separate dining hall, an assembly hall and a head teacher's study are lacking in many schools; 16 per cent of children are at schools which lack four or more of these amenities and only 24 per cent of them are at schools which have them all. Lastly, 28 per cent of the children are taught in schools built on noisy sites.

In addition to giving these material details, the heads supplied figures of the number of pupils who had been eligible to take the secondary selection examinations in the previous year, and the number of successful ones.

All this information refers only to the schools which had one or more of the survey children on their rolls in March 1957. We are only able to describe the last school attended by the 29 per cent of children who changed their primary schools between the ages of eight and eleven.

The middle class parents are highly selective in the primary schools they choose for their children. They are the chief, almost the sole, users of private schools; when they do send their children to maintained schools they favour those that have a reputation for getting a large proportion of their pupils into grammar schools, and those that draw their pupils predominantly from the middle classes. There is a concentration of the best primary schools in the more prosperous residential areas, and to some extent the middle class children go to these schools because they are the nearest ones; there is also an element of choice, for it is those middle class parents who take a great interest in their children's work who are most likely to send them to schools that have a good record of grammar school awards.

The choice of a distant school that has a reputation for getting its pupils into grammar schools, rather than of a nearby one that lacks this reputation, is sometimes possible only because there is a family car. For this reason the opportunities of choice are less for the manual working than for the middle class parents. In general the former send their children to the primary schools that have a poor record of grammar school awards; only 16 per cent of the lower manual working class children go to schools that send 31 per cent or more of pupils to grammar schools, whereas

44 per cent of the upper middle class children attend these schools. On the other hand the educationally ambitious working class parents are more selective in their choice of schools.

In each social class pupils at the academically more successful schools make higher scores than those at the less successful ones; this might, however, be as well explained by the superior quality of the pupils themselves as by the assumption that they are better taught. It is the changes in measured ability rather than the absolute levels that are of relevance here. If it can be shown that the children at the schools with a 'good academic record' improve their performance as they get older, and that this is not explained by the greater incentives given by their parents or by their superior social status, then there is good evidence for suggesting that they have benefited from a superior school environment.

When the eleven-year test scores are compared with the eight-year scores one finds that the children at schools which are favourably assessed draw ahead of the others. This is so whether the schools are judged by their size, their buildings, their amenities, the social background of the pupils, or the past record of grammar school awards. Children at urban schools draw ahead of those at rural ones; those at schools with many amenities draw ahead of those with few; those at large schools draw ahead of those at small; those at schools that recruit their pupils mostly from the middle classes draw ahead of those at schools which recruit their pupils mostly from the manual working classes. The greatest advantages are enjoyed by children at schools with a good record of grammar school awards; for example, those at schools which in the previous year sent 31 per cent or more of 11+ candidates to grammar schools, improve their test scores by an average of 0·85 points between eight and eleven years, whereas those at schools which sent 10 per cent or fewer deteriorate in score by 0·61 points. In other words during these three years the pupils at the most successful schools have gained an average of 1·46 points of test score over the pupils at the least successful schools.[1]

The next problem is to decide which characteristics of the schools, or which combinations of characteristics, are most

[1] Tables XIII(a) and (b), pages 172 and 173.

9

closely related to improvement or deterioration in test performance of the pupils. To look at this, the schools were first
divided into three groups: those with a 'good academic record'
(31 per cent or more of their primary leavers go to grammar
schools), a 'fair record' (11–30 per cent) and a 'poor record'
(10 per cent or less). The changes between eight and eleven
years in the average test performance of the pupils in each group
were then related in turn to the social composition and size of the
schools, the amenities provided and the locality.

When the schools are studied in this way, that is when the
academic record of the school is held constant, the apparent
influence of the other characteristics on test performance is much
reduced. For example, the children at schools which recruit their
pupils predominantly from the middle classes no longer draw
ahead of the children at schools which recruit their pupils predominantly from the unskilled manual working classes, and the
effects of size, locality, and amenities of the schools are similarly
diminished. It seems that the record of previous grammar school
awards provides a better means of forecasting improvement or
deterioration in test performance than does any other charac-
teristic of the primary schools. This view is strengthened if the
procedure is reversed. The advantages of the children at schools
with a good past record over those at schools with a poor one
are virtually unaltered when allowances are made for the fact that
the former are on the average larger, have better buildings, more
amenities and better sites than the latter, and draw a larger
proportion of their pupils from the middle classes.

In the light of these observations, the schools were classified
by their past academic record alone and no account was taken of
their size, amenities, location, or social composition. This classification is, of course, in itself a complex one; many factors in
addition to the standard of teaching contribute to whether a
school sends many or only a few of its pupils to grammar schools;
for example, the average level of ability of the pupils on entry,
the educational ambitions of the parents, and the local availability
of grammar school places.[1] For this reason it was doubtful how

---

[1] It was decided not to adjust the school gradings for the local availability of
grammar school places as our knowledge of local conditions was insufficiently
detailed.

useful this method of classification would be. In the event it has helped to show the part played by primary schools in secondary selection and has indicated the extent to which adverse factors in the home can be offset by good teaching at school. The picture may be blurred, but it is logical and consistent.

It might be thought that the children at schools with a good academic record would draw ahead of the others in the tests of attainment rather than in those of mental ability. For example, if these schools concentrated on the teaching of mechanical arithmetic, the inclusion of an arithmetic test at eleven might give their pupils an advantage over the others. There is indeed some evidence that this is so.[1] The children at the schools with a good academic record owe part of their superior performance in the eleven-year tests to the high scores they make in arithmetic (this test, it will be remembered, replaced the sentence completion test given at eight). This, however, explains only a small part of their increasing advantage in the tests. They pull ahead of the children at the academically less successful schools in every test, and indeed they do so more effectively in the non-verbal intelligence tests than in either the mechanical reading or the vocabulary tests which, being tests of school performance and given moreover in the same form at each age, would have been expected to show the greatest improvement.

The all-round advantage enjoyed by children at schools with a good academic record might be attributed to their greater experience of being tested, but we have no information to show whether or not this is so. Whatever the reason, they have an advantage that increases with age over children from schools with a poor academic record, even when comparisons are made between those who at eight years of age were of the same measured ability. The influence of the primary schools on the level of test performance is relatively small in the lower manual working classes, where those at schools with a good academic record pull ahead of those at schools with a poor one by 0·73 points between eight and eleven years. This compares with 1·34 points for the upper manual workers' children, 1·68 points for the lower middle class children, and 2·98 points for the upper middle class.

[1] Table XIII(c), page 174.

A consistently good record of securing grammar school places in the secondary selection examinations might, of course, be achieved by the schools' concentrating their teaching effort on the clever pupils and leaving the duller ones to get on as best they could. If so the former would improve their performance as compared with children from other schools, whereas the latter might be worse off. It is of interest, then, to see whether the improvement in test performance shown by pupils at schools with a good academic record is equally evident at each level of ability; if it is only evident at the higher levels, one would suspect an element of cramming. It turns out, as is shown in the following table, that the clever children (i.e. those with scores of more than 60 when they are eight years old) who as a group tend to do less well than this in the eleven-year tests[1] show a similar fall in test score whether they are at schools with a good academic record or a poor one. At intermediate levels of ability, which include the majority of children, those at schools with a good academic record have a definite advantage; between eight and eleven years they gain an average of two points over those at schools with a poor record, and their gain is relatively constant at each level of ability above 40 and up to 60. At the bottom end of the scale of measured ability, the backward children with scores of 40 or less make the best progress when they are at schools with a poor academic record.[2]

The pupils who enrol in the schools with a good academic record are a highly selected group—for example, they receive much encouragement from their parents—and the improvement in their average test performance is in part due to this. If one is to assess the influence of the schools themselves, allowances must be made for the different types of pupil they enrol and the different homes they come from. The analysis made by H. R. Simpson was designed to do this. It shows (see page 139) that the academic record of the school, after allowing for the effects of the level of the parents' interest, the size of family and the standard of housing, has relatively little influence on the average

---

[1] This is an example of regression to the mean, a well-known statistical artifact.

[2] It may be that the duller children do badly if they are subjected to intense competition, but the numbers observed in this study are relatively small and this might well be a chance effect.

| Level of measured ability at eight years | Academic Record of School | | |
| | Good | Fair | Poor |
	Change in test score	Change in test score	Change in test score
40 and below	+1·23	+1·67	+2·46
41–45	+1·65	+1·21	−0·41
46–50	+2·61	+1·22	+0·58
51–55	+1·39	+0·76	−0·88
56–60	+0·98	−0·68	−1·76
61 and over	−3·27	−3·18	−3·90

(All figures are standardised for social class)

(+ = improvement   − = deterioration)

test scores of eight-year-old children; this holds for both boys and girls and for the middle as well as for the manual working classes. At this early age the academic record of the school is the least important of the factors examined. At eleven, however, the school has become second in importance to the parents' interest and it is much more important than either housing or family size. It is only among the manual working class boys that it remains throughout of relatively small importance.

These are the answers that would be expected, since eight-year-old children have had relatively little opportunity to be influenced by their teachers; as they get older their teachers have a growing influence which shows itself in school performance and intelligence tests.

When the average test scores of children at these three types of school are adjusted to offset the overlapping effects of parents' interest, size of family and standard of housing, the children at schools with a good past record of 11+ places still have higher average scores and still draw ahead of the rest. The manual working class boys stand out as being little influenced in their test performance by the sort of primary school they attend; at neither eight nor eleven years are they appreciably affected by it.

In the secondary selection examinations, the schools with a good past academic record maintain it and send a higher proportion of their pupils to grammar schools than the remainder.[1] They achieve this because on the one hand their pupils have a higher measured intelligence at eleven, and on the other, the schools themselves tend to be situated in regions of the country where grammar school places are relatively easy to get. Yet even when allowances are made for these factors, their pupils get more places than expected, particularly if they are manual working class children living in areas where grammar school places are in short supply.[2] The greatest benefits fall to those whose measured ability at eleven is on the borderline of the level needed for a grammar school place. At schools with a good academic record 49 per cent of the children who score between 55 and 57 in the eleven-year tests go on to grammar schools, whereas those with a fair or a poor record send only 23 per cent and 11 per cent respectively.

The position may be summarised by saying that children at schools with a good academic record get 20 per cent more grammar school places than their test scores at eleven years would seem to entitle them, whereas those at schools with a fair record get 3 per cent fewer places and those at schools with a poor record get 37 per cent fewer. These figures in each instance make allowances for the social selection of the pupils and the differences in the local availability of grammar school places.

The opportunities for grammar school education among children attending primary schools with a good academic record, come near to the levels wished for by their parents and thought suitable by their teachers. In the other schools opportunities fall below these levels, the discrepancies being greatest for pupils at the schools with a poor academic record. In each type of school, the teachers and mothers make similar assessments and their views are in general agreement with the measured ability of the children.

How far do high standards of teaching in the primary schools make up for lack of interest in the home? This perhaps is the most important question in this book. I have tried to answer it in the

---

[1] Table XIII(d), page 175.
[2] Table XIII(e), page 176.

following way. The survey children were divided according to the academic record of the last school they attended and within each of these types of school by the level of interest—high or low —that their parents showed in their education. The number of grammar school places actually given to these groups of children was then compared with the number that they would have been expected to get, after taking into account their test scores at eight years.

These calculations were made separately for four groups of children, middle class and manual working class living in areas of good and poor provision of grammar school places. The answers for the four calculations were consistent with each other and are combined in the following table.

	Academic Record of Primary School		
	Good	Fair	Poor
	Number of Grammar School Places	Number of Grammar School Places	Number of Grammar School Places
Interested parents:[1]			
Awarded	345	466	54
Expected[2]	347	384	51
Difference	−2	+82	+3
Uninterested parents:			
Awarded	239	296	66
Expected	237	378	69
Difference	+2	−82	−3

[1] This group includes parents showing either a high or an average level of interest.

[2] In calculating the expected numbers at grammar school, eight-year tes score, social class and geographical region were held constant within each type of school.

For children at primary schools with a good academic record, the influence of parental interest on performance in the 11+ examinations is negligible and the same is true for those at schools with a poor record. In contrast, children in the rest of the primary schools (i.e. those which sent between 11 per cent and 30 per cent of their leavers to grammar schools) are influenced by the level of their parents' interest. They get considerably more grammar school places than expected if the level is high whereas those with uninterested parents get less. These observations which compare children of similar ability at eight years imply that between eight and eleven years the deficiencies of parents are being offset by good teaching in the best primary schools, whereas in the worst schools even the children who are encouraged in their work by their parents have no advantage. By improving the level of teaching in the primary schools it seems that the waste of ability through lack of interest and stimulation at home can be much reduced and perhaps eliminated.

The conclusions reached in this chapter are as follows. The primary schools with the best records of grammar school awards attract pupils from the middle classes and those whose parents are anxious for them to succeed. Children at these schools show a relative improvement in their test scores between eight and eleven, so that they draw ahead of the children at the schools which get few grammar school awards. The influence of the school is most marked for the middle class children (both boys and girls) and least marked for the manual working class boys. When the children are eight years the academic success of the schools they are attending has little influence on their test performance, but by the time they are eleven it is very considerable, second only to that of their parents' interest. Over and above this, it affects their chance of going to a grammar school; it exerts its greatest influence on children who are at the borderline level of ability for the award of a grammar school place. It seems that good teaching in the primary schools can make up for deficiencies in parental interest, so that, in the schools with the best record of grammar school awards, the children whose parents take little interest in their school progress do as well as those whose parents take much interest.

The information at our disposal does not allow us to make a more detailed study of the reasons why some primary schools are more successful than others in stimulating their pupils to improve their performance in the tests. One relevant factor, the streaming of children into classes according to their ability, has however, been given special attention and the results are reported in the next chapter.

CHAPTER XIV

Streaming by Ability

So FAR this discussion has centred on various factors which affect the selection of children for secondary schools at 11+; in many primary schools, however, the selective process begins much earlier than this. In the larger schools each age intake of pupils has to be split into several groups or 'streams', so as to make classes of a teachable size. Sometimes this is done by directing the children at random or alphabetically into different groups, in which case these are parallel classes. More often the children are divided up according to their school progress, so that those in the upper streams are the cleverer pupils and those in the lower streams the less able ones. Both types of selection may be followed in the same school; in their early years pupils may be grouped in a random fashion and then, at a later stage, streamed according to their performance in the basic subjects. It seems[1] that the majority of primary school teachers accept that streaming by ability or attainment is educationally sound, and believe that the less able children in particular benefit from being taught in classes made up of children of similar ability. There is some indirect evidence that this is so for reading.[2]

It has been suggested[3] that when selection is by ability, there is a tendency to place middle class children in the top streams because they have learnt in their homes to use words with precision; once there they receive continuing verbal training, which maintains their initial superiority and, at later ages, gives them a further advantage in tests. The manual working class children, on the other hand, who were in the first place put in the lower streams because they lacked the initial stimulation at home are then further deprived by being given a relatively unacademic type of education at school. This is an extreme statement of the

[1] Daniels, J. C. (1961).
[2] Morris, J. M. (1959).
[3] Davis, A. (1951).

social bias that might be implicit in early selection by ability; that it is not entirely without foundation will be seen below.

There is no clear evidence that children either benefit or suffer from being streamed. A recent study[1] compared children at unstreamed junior schools with children of similar intellectual ability from streamed schools; the unstreamed children drew ahead of the streamed children in tests of intelligence and of school subjects and there was a suggestion that the backward benefited more from non-streaming than the brighter children. This study is, however, open to the criticism that the teaching methods in the non-streamed schools may have been more 'consistently thought-out' than in the streamed schools. In the absence of specific plans for changing the content and methods of teaching so as to provide the most challenging learning situations for each group of pupils, it seems that ability grouping does not make an appreciable difference to the average level of performance.[2]

A special study was made in this survey of the children in two-stream schools. With the generous help of the Directors of Education it was possible to separate out a group of children who were streamed by ability before their eighth birthday and who had stayed in the same schools from then until they sat the 11 + selection examinations. During these years they continued to be streamed by ability into one or other of two classes.

There were, in all, 491 children in two-stream schools who satisfied these requirements;[3] 62 per cent were in the upper or A stream at eight years and 38 per cent in the lower or B stream.

It was rare for children to change streams; over the whole three-year period the annual rate of transfer was 2·3 per cent and approximately the same numbers moved up as down. On this showing the system of streaming by ability is more rigid than is generally realised; for example, when, in another study, teachers in three-streamed schools were asked to estimate the proportion

---

[1] Daniels, J. C. (1961).

[2] Goldberg, M. L., *et al.* (1961).

[3] In order to isolate these children it was necessary to obtain additional information which not all the Local Education Authorities could provide; the total of 491 children is an underestimate of the number in the whole sample in two-stream schools classified by ability at eight years and not changing school thereafter.

of pupils who were promoted or demoted, they gave on the average a figure of 19 per cent changes each year,[1] which is more than seven times as large as the rate of change recorded in the present survey. The schools themselves also tended to give higher figures; in the same study, returns from twenty-seven three-stream primary schools showed an average annual rate of transfer of 6 per cent. Perhaps there are more transfers in three-stream than in two-stream schools, or perhaps in these three-stream schools children who left or joined late were confounded with those who changed their streams.

As judged by their performance in the eight-year tests, the survey children in the upper streams are of considerably higher ability (55·44 average T score) than those in the lower streams (44·72), though there is, of course, a very decided overlap in the test scores of individual children in these two streams.[2]

During the succeeding three years the children in the upper streams improve their scores by an average of 0·71 points and those in the lower streams deteriorate by 0·49 points. In the upper streams, moreover, the standard deviation (or spread of the test scores) is 17 per cent less in the eleven-year tests than in the eight; the less clever children in these streams have improved more than the brighter ones so that the class members have drawn closer together in measured ability by the time they are eleven. The children in the lower streams on the other hand show virtually the same range of variation in measured ability at eleven years as at eight.

At each level of ability the children in the upper streams improve their scores while the others deteriorate. In the upper streams it is particularly the children of relatively low ability who benefit—those, for example, with scores between 41 and 51 improve by an average of 4·5 points, whereas those with scores between 52 and 60 improve by only 1·3 points. In the lower streams, the brighter children show a greater average deterioration in test score (2·7 points) than the duller children (0·9 points). It seems then, that the less able children in the upper streams are stimulated by high standards of teaching or by the competition of brighter children, whereas in the lower streams

[1] Daniels, J. C. (1961).
[2] Table XIV(a), page 177.

the relatively bright children are handicapped either by unsuitable teaching or lack of competition. The figures which are given in the following table suggest why transfers between streams are so rare; once allocated, the children tend to take on the characteristics expected of them and the forecasts of ability made at the point of streaming are to this extent self-fulfilling.

Measured ability at eight years	Stream	
	Upper	Lower
	Change in score 8–11 years	Change in score 8–11 years
41–45	+5·67	−0·95
46–48	+3·70	−0·62
49–51	+4·44	−1·60
52–54	+0·71	−1·46
55–57	+2·23	−1·94
58–60	+0·86	−6·34

(+ = improvement   − = deterioration)

The expressed intention of the teachers was to stream these children according to their measured ability, but in the early years at primary school it seems that judgements of ability are influenced by the types of home. It is, of course, expected that there would be a greater proportion of middle class children in the upper than in the lower streams, because of their higher average measured ability. The inequalities observed are, however, greater than this for even when children of the same level of ability are considered, the middle class children tend to be allocated to the upper streams and the manual working class children to the lower ones (there are 11 per cent more middle class children in the upper streams than would be expected from their measured ability at eight years and 26 per cent fewer in the lower). These figures probably underestimate the extent of social selection in streaming, as they do not take account of any changes in performance that may have occurred in the interval between the time when the children were streamed and when they took the eight-year tests.

The standard of maternal care given to these children during the pre-school years has a greater influence than social class on their chances of being put into the upper streams. Those who during the first six years of their lives were said to be dirty, badly clothed and shod are likely to be found in the lower streams. In these streams there are 29 per cent of children with a history of poor maternal care in infancy, when only 21 per cent would have been expected.[1] In the upper streams 10 per cent had a similar history, whereas 14 per cent would have been expected. This tendency to put the poorly cared for children into the lower streams is more marked in the lower ranges of ability, but is found to some degree at each level of test score. Associated with it, as is shown in the following table, is a marked tendency to put children from large families into the lower streams.

Test score at eight years	% with Poor Maternal Care		% from Large Families	
	Upper Stream	Lower Stream	Upper Stream	Lower Stream
41–45	nil	42·1	33·3	64·4
46–48	12·0	20·0	40·0	58·1
49–51	15·2	35·7	38·9	46·7
52–60	9·9	12·5	39·0	60·0

The parents with children in the lower streams visit the schools as often and are regarded by the teachers as being just as interested in their children's progress as the parents of those in the upper. The former group of parents, as might be expected, is less eager for their children to go to grammar schools, and in this they may well be trimming their expectations to reality, for it is rare for a child in a lower stream to get a grammar school place. On the basis of measured ability at eight years, twelve of the children in the lower streams should have gone to grammar schools, but only one in fact did so.

[1] Expected, that is to say, after taking account of their level of measured ability at eight years.

The effects of streaming on educational opportunity extend beyond the point of secondary selection. The children from the lower streams are likely to leave early; 82 per cent of them left at fifteen as compared with an expected 76 per cent, whereas from the upper streams 39 per cent left at fifteen, as compared with an expected 46 per cent.[1]

So far, only those who remained in the same stream from the age of eight to eleven have been considered. The few children who moved from the lower to the upper streams are distinguished by having received superior care in early childhood, by being of higher measured ability at eight and by improving their test performance between eight and eleven years (0·95 points) as compared with a deterioration of 0·49 points observed among the children who remained in the lower streams. The children who start in the upper streams and end in the lower tend to be those from large families who received poor care in early childhood; their average score at eight years was nearer to that of children in the lower streams than in the upper, and although they improved their scores between eight and eleven years by 0·15 points, this is less than a quarter of the improvement recorded for the pupils who remained in the upper streams throughout. While the reallocation of streams reinforces the original selection by ability, it also in a minor way continues the selective process which favours the children who are well cared for in early childhood.

Both the middle and the manual working class children improve their average test scores between eight and eleven if they are in the upper streams, but the former show a much greater rate of improvement than the latter (1·63 points as compared with 0·48). Similarly in the lower streams, the middle class children improve their scores between eight and eleven years by 0·78 points, whereas the manual working class children deteriorate by 1·05 points. From this it seems that the manual working class children are affected in a different way from the middle class by the process of streaming, and that they show in particular a severe deterioration in performance if they are put in the lower streams.

[1] Again these figures compare pupils of similar measured ability in the two streams. (See also footnote 2, page 124.)

The criticisms made in this chapter are aimed at the unconscious biases of selection rather than at the concept of streaming. The teachers, it seems, accept streaming as desirable and so, in the absence of a carefully thought-out policy of non-streaming which has the enthusiastic support of the teachers committed to it, it is likely that children will make better academic progress in streamed than in unstreamed schools. This, which is of course no justification of streaming by ability, is true of the present sample of children.[1] There is in fact no basis of comparison provided by the present study, since the unstreamed schools tend to be the small ones with the least satisfactory records of past academic success, often drawing their pupils from rural homes. What is needed is a planned experiment of the effects of streaming, and this is very different from the simple description we have been able to provide.

In summary, streaming by ability reinforces the process of social selection which was observed in the earlier chapters of this book. Children who come from well-kept homes and who are themselves clean, well clothed and shod, stand a greater chance of being put in the upper streams than their measured ability would seem to justify. Once there they are likely to stay and to improve in performance in succeeding years. This is in striking contrast to the deterioration noticed in those children of similar initial measured ability who were placed in the lower streams. In this way the validity of the initial selection appears to be confirmed by the subsequent performance of the children, and an element of rigidity is introduced early into the primary school system.

[1] Table XIV(*b*), page 178.

CHAPTER XV

Wastage of Ability

THE evidence set out in this book gives strong reasons for believing that much potential ability is wasted during the primary school years and misdirected at the point of secondary selection. It is the purpose of this final chapter to examine the following questions, which have a bearing on the interpretation of these results.

(*a*) Do the environmental factors act independently of each other in producing changes in test score?

(*b*) How far do later transfers to grammar schools, and the award of technical school places to manual working class children, make up for the relatively few grammar school places given to them in the secondary selection examinations?

(*c*) How far does private schooling contribute to the social inequalities in education?

(*d*) Supposing that middle class attitudes to education spread through the community, how far would demand for selective secondary school places expand?

(*e*) Is the estimate of educational wastage made in this book, which is based on grammar school awards, a realistic one in the context of early leaving?

(*a*) *How far do environmental factors act independently?*

This question concerns the changes in test score which were recorded in earlier chapters: children from good homes and schools improve their test performance between eight and eleven years, whereas children from poor homes and schools deteriorate. What evidence is there that the homes and schools each have a direct effect on the test performance of the children? We might be recording no more than differences in the sensitivity of the tests used at eight and eleven years; or we might be attributing effects to these separate environmental factors, which should rather be attributed to some more distant factor with which they are all correlated, but which it has not been possible to isolate.

10

In either event a grey uniformity would be expected in the results, which is certainly not found. Indeed the effects of each of the factors are exerted at the time and in the direction that would have been predicted. Take, for example, the academic record of primary schools. The quality of teaching has had a smaller chance to influence the progress of the eight-year-old than the eleven-year-old children, and from this it would be predicted that the type of school a child goes to has an increasingly important influence on his performance, as he grows older. This is so; the schools' academic record, from being the least important of the four factors studied at eight, becomes the second most important at eleven. The findings for the other factors studied are similarly predictable, and further evidence that they are acting independently of each other lies in the absence of any significant first order interaction. (See page 135.)

Taken as a whole, this study provides strong evidence that between the ages of eight and eleven the performance of children in tests of mental ability and school achievement is greatly influenced by their homes and schools, influenced moreover in a predictable way. No claim is made that these tests measure innate ability; on the contrary, three out of the four given at each age were designed to measure the level of achievement in school subjects. All that has been shown is that a child's capacity to do well in his work at school is to a certain degree dependent on the encouragement he gets from his parents, the sort of home he has and the academic record of his school. The full influence of these factors on performance cannot be measured because tests were not given until the children were eight years old. But even if their influence is no greater than that suggested by the changes in score noted between eight and eleven years, which is unlikely, this represents an avoidable loss of ability which no system of selective examinations at eleven can eliminate, and which is likely to continue to lead to further loss through early leaving and academic failure in the secondary schools.

(b) Do late transfers to grammar schools or the award of technical school places reduce the social inequalities of 11+ selection?

It has been estimated that, 'even the use of best methods of allocation that, on the basis of our present knowledge can be devised is likely to involve errors in the allocation of approximately 10 per cent of the candidates'.[1] Yet transfers from secondary modern to grammar schools are rare and are, in any case, largely a matter of filling the vacant desks left by pupils who have moved from grammar to other types of school. In so far as they effect the social class differences in educational opportunity, they increase rather than diminish them.[2] The highest proportion of transfers is in the upper middle class, the lowest in the lower manual working class; indeed, of the pupils who do transfer, half come from the middle classes, and this is a far larger proportion than would be expected by chance.

The earlier description of the hazards of secondary selection took no account of the award of places in technical schools. The reason for this omission is that a considerable number of children do not reach these schools until they are thirteen years old; the results of the selection examinations give, therefore, only an imperfect account of the part played by these schools in secondary education. In 1961 we obtained further details of schooling, and so are also able to look at the technical school awards. A total of 5·2 per cent of fourteen-year-olds were in technical schools and the question is how far shortages of grammar school places are offset by increased opportunity at the technical school level.

It could be argued that social class differences in educational opportunity are less than they appear in this study, for although manual working class children get fewer grammar school places than their measured ability would entitle them to, they largely make up for this disadvantage by the greater number of places they obtain in technical schools. Even if the technical schools are regarded as the equivalent of grammar schools, the manual working class children are still less well provided for than the upper middle class children of similar measured ability. Those in the lower manual working classes, for example, get only 85 per cent as many places in grammar and technical schools as do an equivalent group of upper middle class children.[3] The lower manual

---

[1] Yates, A., and Pidgeon, D. A. (1957).

[2] Table XV(a), page 179, shows the proportion of fifteen-year-old children at grammar schools.

[3] See Table XV(b), page 180.

working class boys do better; they get 98 per cent of the places that would be expected for a group of upper middle class boys of equivalent measured ability, whereas the lower manual working class girls get only 73 per cent.

If these figures are regarded as showing equality of educational opportunity for the boys, it can be only in a very special and highly restricted and restrictive sense. In the upper middle class there are fourteen pupils in grammar schools for every one in a technical school, whereas in the lower manual working class, there are only two pupils in grammar schools for every one in a technical school. This is a distribution of selective secondary school places that can hardly be justified in terms of social equity or, for that matter, of national interest. Why should a level of ability which leads in one social class to the grammar schools and the universities, lead in another to the technical schools with restricted opportunities for further education and a pattern of early leaving?

(c) How far does private schooling contribute to social inequalities in education?

The independent secondary schools were left out of these calculations because, as with technical schools, a number of children transfer to them after the age of eleven, and it is not for a year or so after this that the whole extent of private secondary education is known. When the criterion of selective secondary education is broadened to include private as well as grammar and technical schools, all semblance of social equality vanishes.[1] Comparing children of equal measured ability at eleven, those from the upper middle class get three times as many selective school places as those from the lower manual, more than twice as many as those from the upper manual and one and a half times as many as those from the lower middle class.

It may be thought that the upper middle class parents are over-investing in education, that they are giving a superior education to children who are not clever enough to benefit from it. Certainly at the higher ranges of measured ability (T scores of 61 and over) lower manual working class children are as likely to enter selective secondary schools, as children from any

[1] Table XV(c), page 181.

other social class. It is only at lower levels of ability that their opportunities are restricted and that social inequalities are pronounced. This is shown in the following table.

Test scores at eleven years	Middle Class		Manual Working Class	
	Upper	Lower	Upper	Lower
	% at Selective Secondary School	% at Selective Secondary School	% at Selective Secondary School	% at Selective Secondary School
54 or less	40·1	17·0	10·2	7·9
55–60	80·3	65·9	49·8	51·6
61 and over	99·0	93·9	96·3	92·3

Perhaps the middle class children who go to selective secondary schools have special qualities of character that later help them to succeed in their studies, even when their performance in tests given at the age of eleven is below that needed for grammar or technical school entry. This is no justification for social class inequalities in the distribution of selective secondary school places. These educationally desirable qualities of character are hardly likely to be inborn and limited to the middle classes, and if we are to make full use of the potential talent of the nation's children, they should be fostered in all social classes.

It seems that a substantial proportion of the potentially clever children are today not reaching the selective secondary schools. When ability is judged by the eleven-year test score, 26·8 per cent of children with scores of 55 or over, and 5·0 per cent with scores of 60 or over, go to secondary modern schools; when ability is judged by the eight-year scores the equivalent percentages rise to 33·1 per cent and 16·6 per cent.

(d) How far is the demand for selective secondary school places likely

to expand as middle class attitudes to education spread through the community?

In order to answer this question it is necessary to see how far social inequalities in the distribution of secondary school places alter when the ability of children is judged by their test performance at eight rather than at eleven. During their last three years at primary school the middle class children pull ahead of the manual working class in test performance; for this reason inequalities in the distribution of selective secondary school places are much greater when the eight-year test scores are used as the measure of ability. Taking the award of grammar school places in the upper middle classes as the standard to be aimed at, 1,005[1] children who ought by their eight-year test scores to have got places failed to do so. When the eleven-year test scores are used as the criterion of ability this figure of loss is reduced to 595. To meet this deficit the number of grammar school places should be increased by 56 per cent if the eight-year tests are the criterion, or 32 per cent if the eleven year.

So far only grammar school places have been considered. If the upper middle class attitudes diffuse through the community to the extent that similar demands are made by all classes for selective school places of all types, an increase of 75 per cent would be required. To satisfy this demand we should have to provide selective secondary schools for 47 per cent of all children.[2]

(e) Is the estimate of educational waste supported by the facts of early leaving?

Further information on school progress was obtained at fifteen years, and it is possible now to look at the proportion who left school at the earliest age. This gives another estimate of educational loss which shows the number of high ability who are lost from secondary education at an early age. While some of them may, on leaving, enter full-time further education courses, these will be mainly of a commercial and non-academic type.

Sixty-four per cent of the survey group left school when they were fifteen,[3] the great majority of course from secondary

---

[1] These are population estimates. They refer to the position at fifteen years.

[2] This calculation is based on the eight-year tests.

[3] More correctly their teachers just before their fifteenth birthday said that they were leaving at the end of the term.

modern schools or streams. The proportion who left at fifteen varies from 16 per cent in the upper middle class families to 77 per cent in the lower manual working class, and this difference is by no means wholly explained by variations in the level of measured ability. In the upper middle class only 0·6 per cent of those with T score at eleven of 61 or more leave at fifteen, whereas 12·8 per cent of the equivalent group from the lower manual working class leave at this age. This is shown in the following table.

| | Middle Class | | Manual Working Class | |
| | Upper | Lower | Upper | Lower |
Eleven-year test score	% leaving school at fifteen	% leaving school at fifteen	% leaving school at fifteen	% leaving school at fifteen
54 or less	35·6	72·6	80·0	89·3
55–60	12·6	23·4	32·1	40·0
61 and over	0·6	3·4	2·6	12·8
All	16·5	46·4	62·3	77·4

Those leaving at the earliest possible moment include 20·7 per cent of the children who score 55 and over in the eleven-year tests and 27·7 per cent of those who made similar scores in the eight-year tests. The majority of these youngsters of above average ability come from the manual working classes. At this level of ability it would be generally agreed that fifteen is too early an age to leave school. This is not a situation that need be accepted. In regions such as Wales where the provision of grammar school places is relatively high, fewer of these children leave school early; of the manual working class children who score 55–60 in the eleven-year tests only 30 per cent leave school early in these regions as compared with 42 per cent of similar children in those where grammar school places are in short supply; in the middle classes the equivalent figures are 17 per cent and 23 per cent. Undoubtedly, as more grammar school places become available, so early leaving among the relatively able will be reduced.

It is probable that early leaving will be less widespread in the future. If youngsters from all social classes at each separate level of ability were as likely to stay on at school after fifteen as those of the upper middle class, then early losses would be reduced from 54 per cent of those scoring 43 and over at eleven[1] to 29 per cent, and the losses of the more able ones (scoring 55 and over at eleven) from 21 per cent to 9 per cent.

.   .   .

A detailed study of school leaving is outside the scope of this book. The pattern in Scotland does, however, need to be described. Scottish children have so far been excluded from this study because they are selected for secondary schools at a different age and in a different manner from the English and Welsh. When it comes to school leaving, however, valid comparisons related to measured ability may be made of educational loss North and South of the Border. That early leaving is relatively common in Scotland, even in the selective secondary schools, is evident from Macpherson's study.[2] The reputation of Scottish education is high and it is unexpected to find that early leaving is more the pattern there than in the South. It is not just that more of the less able leave; the greatest difference between Scotland and the rest of Britain is found among youngsters who are above the average in measured ability (52–60 T score). These findings cannot be explained by differences in the social and educational background of the parents, since in each social class (except the upper middle in which there are only 44 Scottish children) the proportion of early leavers is higher in Scotland than in England and Wales, the greatest difference being observed in the upper manual working class.

Macpherson says, 'it is obviously very difficult to use the word "wastage" in connection with some of the boys who left

[1] There are too few scoring below 43 in the upper middle class to allow the calculation of a reliable proportion of early leavers at this level of ability.

[2] Macpherson, J. (1958).

	Level of Test Score at Eight Years		
	51 *or less*	52–60	61 *or more*
	% *leaving school at fifteen*	% *leaving school at fifteen*	% *leaving school at fifteen*
England and Wales	74·4	43·8	15·6
Scotland	89·6	58·3	17·4

before completing the course . . .' and he reports that many of those who left the five-year courses in Scottish senior secondary schools had not been succeeding in their studies and were lacking in certain important personality characteristics. It seems that this too holds for the early leavers in England and Wales[1]— they tend to be rated as lazy or poor workers in the primary schools, to show a fall in level of test performance between eight and eleven, and to be rated adversely by their teachers. Perhaps it is true to say that 'not all of the potential ability in an age group could be realised in practice'; but the different pattern of leaving in Scotland and the rest of Britain (for that matter, between different parts of England and Wales) shows that there is at present no justification for a smug acceptance of this view, and every reason for dissatisfaction with the results of our efforts to keep pupils at school.

In recent discussions there has been a tendency to assume that there is only a limited number of persons who can benefit from higher education and that there is a clearly defined 'pool of talent' on which to draw for university places. It has been said, however, that what is extracted from the pool depends much less on its content than on the effectiveness of the pump; it is clear from the present study that the pump is leaking badly at the points of secondary selection and school leaving.

The pool of talent found at the end of the secondary school period is likely to be only a portion of that which would be found

[1] This comment is based on a preliminary scrutiny of the data which will be described fully in another publication.

if it were possible to draw fully on potential rather than realised ability. Over a period of three years in the primary schools, there is a substantial loss of ability in the manual working class children which could be prevented, it seems, by better teaching, even if the attitude of working class parents towards education does not change. If our aim is to preserve the pool of talent it may be more important to improve the level of teaching in the primary than in the secondary schools. The problem goes beyond this, however, for it is likely that in the pre-school years the mental development of many children is stunted by the intellectual poverty of their surroundings. Here is a wide field for study. Perhaps we should think in terms of nursery schools which aim to give small children the stimulus that is so often lacking in their homes. But the first need is to measure more fully the impact of the family on the early processes of learning and on the acquisition of incentives before children reach school.

Tests Used in 1954 and 1957 Surveys

D. A. PIDGEON

National Foundation for Educational Research in England and Wales

MAINLY due to considerations of time and the fact that, in the majority of cases, the tests would be given individually by teachers relatively inexperienced in this kind of testing, the choice of tests to be given in the survey was severely limited. At age eight, and at eleven, four tests were given, in each case combined into a single booklet complete with full details for administration and scoring. Considerable care was taken in compiling the booklets so that the task of the teachers giving the tests was as straightforward as possible. A number of Local Authorities, however, made arrangements for the testing to be carried out either by psychologists or by other trained personnel. The total testing time at each age was under two hours, and the testing, in all but a few instances, was spread over two or three mornings. Although the tests were scored by the person giving the tests, they were all re-marked at the National Foundation. Norms were calculated from the data obtained and raw scores converted to T-scores with a mean of 50 and standard deviation 10.

1954 *Testing*

The four tests given at age eight were:

1. A 60-item non-verbal picture test. Published by the N.F.E.R. as Picture Test 1 by J. E. Stuart.

2. A 35-item reading comprehension test. Published by the N.F.E.R. as Sentence Reading Test 1 by A. F. Watts.

3. A 50-item mechanical word reading test. ⎱ The same list of words was used in both these tests, which were also

4. A 50-item vocabulary test. ⎰ given at eleven years.

Reliability of the Tests

Although a comparison of the mean and range of test scores obtained from children tested on the one hand by teachers and on the other by psychologists or other experienced testers, revealed no differences, because of the nature of the testing it was decided to investigate the question of reliability by arranging for the administration of the test battery on two occasions to the same group of children. All children attaining the age of eight between the 1st and 7th of July, 1956, in a large County Borough were used for the experiment. 124 children were given the tests under the same conditions as in the survey, during the week 11th–15th June, 1956, and were subsequently re-tested in the period 2nd–13th July, 1956. The teachers concerned had not been informed that the testing was to be repeated. 108 children completed all four tests on both occasions and the test-retest correlations were as follows:

	Picture Test	Reading Comp. Test	Mech. Reading	Vocabulary
Test–retest reliability	·86	·90	·96	·87

In view of the conditions under which the tests were administered these reliabilities must be considered satisfactory. A separate value of the reliability of the Picture Test by group administration has been calculated from a sample of 200 scripts by Kuder-Richardson Formula 20 to be 0·92. Also a separate test-retest correlation with group administration one week apart has been calculated for Sentence Reading Test 1 on a small group of 49 children aged 7:6 to 8:1 and found to be 0·94.

No direct data on the validity of the tests at this age have been obtained, but the test inter-correlations obtained from the survey are as follows:

	Reading Comp. Test	Mech. Reading Test	Vocabulary Test
Picture Test	·56	·53	·57
Reading Comprehension Test		·87	·68
Mechanical Reading Test			·69

1957 *Testing*

The tests used at age eleven were:

1. An 80-item verbal and non-verbal   Alternate items verbal and
   ability test.   non-verbal.
2. A 50-item arithmetic test.   20 mechanical sums and
                                        30 problems.
3. A 50-item mechanical word read- ⎫ The same two tests used
   ing test.   ⎬ in the survey at age
4. A 50-item vocabulary test.   ⎭ eight.

Reliability of the Tests

The reliabilities of the four tests used have been calculated as follows:

1. Verbal and Non-Verbal Test.   Kuder-Richardson   (N = 363)   ·94
                                 Formula 20
2. Arithmetic Test.   Kuder-Richardson   (N = 361)   ·96
                                 Formula 20
3. Mechanical Reading Test.   Split-half   (N = 357)   ·96
4. Vocabulary Test.   Split-half   (N = 357)   ·92

Although partially 'power' tests, both the Verbal and Non-Verbal Test and the Arithmetic Test were timed and hence the values for the reliabilities obtained are likely to be slight over-estimates. The figures, nevertheless, can be considered satisfactory.

Validities

Direct evidence on the validity of tests such as these is difficult to obtain. However, the four tests were given to a group of 74 children in the fourth year of their primary school, who had also been given three eleven-plus selection tests—National Foundation Verbal Test 8A, English Test 8 and Arithmetic Test 8. The correlations obtained were as follows:

Verbal and Non-Verbal Test with Verbal Test 8A	·93
Arithmetic Test with Arithmetic Test 8	·95
Mechanical Reading Test with English Test 8	·89
Vocabulary Test with English Test 8	·86

Another National Foundation Survey Reading Test (N.S.6) was also given to the children in the group. It correlated ·90 with the survey mechanical reading test and ·86 with the vocabulary test.

The mechanical reading test and the vocabulary test were given on both occasions of testing, in 1954 and 1957. Inter-correlations over the three-year interval were as follows:

	Mechanical Reading 1957	Vocabulary 1957
Mechanical Reading 1954	·79	·66
Vocabulary 1954	·62	·71

It is of interest also to report the inter-correlations obtained from the survey data:

	Arithmetic Test	Mech. Reading Test	Vocabulary Test
Verbal and Non-Verbal Test	·75	·69	·69
Arithmetic Test		·69	·65
Mechanical Reading Test			·77

The Influence of Home and School on Test Performance

H. R. SIMPSON

Rothamsted Experimental Station

THE analysis of the test scores at eight and eleven years is complicated by the unequal number of children in the thirty-six subclasses determined by the factors:

(a) Housing
(b) Academic record of primary school
(c) Completed family size
(d) Parents' interest[1]

This situation is commonly found in survey data, where the research worker has no control over the composition of the sample (except by resort to quota sampling).

In such cases the design is said to be non-orthogonal and the standard methods of estimation and analysis of variance cannot be applied. The statistical technique for handling non-orthogonal

---

[1] The levels of these four factors are as follows:

Housing. Two levels, 'satisfactory' and 'unsatisfactory', based on assessments of crowding, bed-sharing and amenities throughout the primary school years and defined on page 35.

Academic record of primary school. Three levels. In the year preceding 1957, the schools with a 'good' record sent 31 per cent or more of their leavers to grammar schools, those with a 'fair' record sent 11–30 per cent and those with a 'poor' record less than 11 per cent. (See page 104.)

Completed family size. Three levels. 1 or 2 children born up to March 1957, 3 children born up to March 1957, 4 or more children born up to March 1957.

Parents' interest. Two levels. The 'interested' parents are those assessed (see page 54) as taking a high or fair level of interest in their children's progress at school. The 'less interested' parents are those taking a low level of interest.

data was described by Yates,[1] and a method of overcoming the computational difficulties involved was given by Stevens.[2] This method, slightly modified, has been programmed by Yates for the Elliott–N.R.D.C. 401 electronic computer at Rothamsted; the numerical results presented in this appendix were calculated on the 401.

Consider, for simplicity, data classified by two factors A and B only, with subclasses A_1, $A_2 \ldots A_i \ldots$ and B_1, $B_2 \ldots B_j \ldots$ The simplest model that may be postulated is

$$y_{ij} = m + a_i + b_j + \text{error} \quad \ldots\ldots\ldots\ldots (1)$$

i.e. the observation on the $(i,j)^{\text{th}}$ subclass is composed of a general mean, two independent contributions from the factors, and a residual error term. If this model is not valid, the factors are said to interact, and a model of the form

$$y_{ij} = m + c_{ij} + \text{error} \quad \ldots\ldots\ldots\ldots (2)$$

is required, where different constants are fitted to each subgroup. To determine whether model (2) is necessary the mean square for interaction should be compared with the residual mean square after fitting model (2).

Because of the non-orthogonality of the design, the mean square due to factor A cannot be directly obtained, and it must be derived from the difference between the—

> Sum of squares due to fitting A and B together
> (i.e. fitting model (1)) and the—
> Sum of squares due to fitting B alone, ignoring A
> (i.e. fitting the model $y_{ij} = m + b_j + \text{error}$)

This difference is the sum of squares for A (eliminating B), and the corresponding mean square should be tested against the residual mean square obtained when fitting model (1).

The National Survey Data

The analyses of variance for the four groups, middle class and

[1] Yates, F. 'The Analysis of Multiple Classifications with unequal numbers in the different classes', *J. American Statist. Assoc.* 29 (1934), 51–56.

[2] Stevens, W. L. 'Statistical Analysis of a non-orthogonal tri-factorial experiment', *Biometrika* 35 (1948), 346–367.

manual working class boys and girls, are shown in Table A. In no case is the interaction mean square significant: the largest ratio is 1·72, whereas the 5 per cent point of the F distribution with 13 and 16 d.f. is 2·4.

The relative importance of the factors can be assessed from their associated mean squares which are also given in Table A. The meaning of these results is discussed in the main body of the book.

The remaining tables on pages 136 to 139 give the adjusted means for each category of the main factors. The means are adjusted in that the effect of other factors is eliminated, the values given being the expected marginal means when constants for all main effects are fitted.

This analysis was based on the sample numbers and not on the population estimates.

TABLE A—ANALYSIS OF VARIANCE

Mean squares for each factor, eliminating the others.

	Degrees of freedom	Mean Square Middle class boys		Mean Square Middle class girls	
		8-yr. tests	11-yr. tests	8-yr. tests	11-yr. tests
Parents' interest	1	1500·9	1758·1	962·0	1758·8
Housing	1	663·9	424·2	711·0	389·6
Completed family size	2	217·0	435·2	207·6	130·7
Academic record of school	2	137·5	472·6	264·9	580·8
All main effects	6	746·0	1012·6	560·6	742·2
Residual	29	36·4	49·8	69·7	62·0
First order interactions	13	47·4	60·4	56·0	75·1
Residual	16	27·5	41·2	80·8	51·4

	Degrees of freedom	Mean Square Manual working class boys		Mean Square Manual working class girls	
		8-yr. tests	11-yr. tests	8-yr. tests	11-yr. tests
Parents' interest	1	1367·8	1914·7	1744·8	3245·4
Housing	1	538·0	794·3	93·6	364·0
Completed family size	2	506·6	491·3	633·2	486·7
Academic record of school	2	70·4	209·4	330·3	607·4
All main effects	6	792·9	1051·8	965·8	1464·7
Residual	29	68·1	67·4	62·2	70·9
First order interactions	13	62·4	50·2	70·0	88·6
Residual	16	72·8	81·4	55·9	56·6

TABLE B—TESTS OF SIGNIFICANCE

	Degrees of freedom	F ratios Middle Class Boys		F ratios Middle Class Girls	
		8-yr. tests	11-yr. tests	8-yr. tests	11-yr. tests
Parents' interest	1,29	41·2*	35·3*	13·8*	28·4*
Housing	1,29	18·2*	8·5*	10·2*	6·3†
Completed family size	2,29	6·0*	8·7*	3·0	2·1
Academic record of school	2,29	3·8†	9·5*	3·8†	9·4*

	Degrees of freedom	F ratios Manual working class boys		F ratios Manual working class girls	
		8-yr. tests	11-yr. tests	8-yr. tests	11-yr. tests
Parents' interest	1,29	20·1*	28·4*	28·0*	45·7*
Housing	1,29	7·9*	11·8*	1·5	5·1†
Completed family size	2,29	7·4*	7·3*	10·2*	6·9*
Academic record of school	2,29	1·0	3·1	5·3†	8·6*

The statistical significance of these figures is shown as follows:

* $\quad$ P < 0·01 = highly significant
† $\quad$ 0·05 > P > 0·01 = significant
otherwise $\quad$ P > 0·05 = not significant

Table C—PARENTS' INTEREST

8- and 11-year test scores (adjusted means)

	Boys		Girls	
	8-yrs.	*11-yrs.*	*8-yrs.*	*11-yrs.*
Middle class:				
Interested parents	56·0	57·5	56·2	57·4
Less interested parents	52·7	53·9	53·3	53·5
Difference	3·3	3·6	2·9	3·9
Manual working class:				
Interested parents	51·3	51·3	52·0	52·6
Less interested parents	47·9	47·2	48·4	47·7
Difference	3·4	4·1	3·6	4·9

Table D—HOUSING

8- and 11-year test scores (adjusted means)

	Boys		Girls	
	8-yrs.	*11-yrs.*	*8-yrs.*	*11-yrs.*
Middle class:				
Satisfactory housing	55·3	56·5	55·9	56·4
Unsatisfactory housing	52·9	54·5	53·2	54·4
Difference	2·4	2·0	2·7	2·0
Manual working class:				
Satisfactory housing	50·2	50·0	50·0	50·2
Unsatisfactory housing	48·1	47·4	49·2	48·6
Difference	2·1	2·6	0·8	1·6

TABLE E—COMPLETED FAMILY SIZE

8- and 11-year test scores (adjusted means)

	Boys		Girls	
	8-yrs.	11-yrs.	8-yrs.	11-yrs.
Middle class:				
1 or 2 child families	55·0	56·9	55·7	56·3
3 child families	55·0	54·8	53·5	54·6
4 or more child families	52·6	53·8	55·2	56·0
Difference	2·4	3·1	0·5	0·3
Manual working class:				
1 or 2 child families	49·9	49·2	50·7	50·1
3 child families	49·3	49·0	49·9	49·9
4 or more child families	47·0	46·5	47·4	47·3
Difference	2·9	2·7	3·3	2·8

TABLE F—ACADEMIC RECORD OF SCHOOL

8- and 11-year test scores (adjusted means)

	Boys		Girls	
	8-yrs.	11-yrs.	8-yrs.	11-yrs.
Middle class:				
Good academic record	55·6	57·7	56·2	57·5
Fair academic record	54·2	55·4	54·7	55·3
Poor academic record	53·6	54·0	53·1	52·8
Difference	2·0	3·7	3·1	4·7
Manual working class:				
Good academic record	48·9	48·8	51·4	51·7
Fair academic record	49·0	48·6	49·4	49·1
Poor academic record	48·0	46·9	48·4	47·6
Difference	0·9	1·9	3·0	4·1

APPENDIX III

Tables

THE tables are grouped for convenience under the chapter headings.

Unless otherwise stated all figures are population estimates, that is to say, the manual working class children (except those of the agricultural workers) and those of the employers and self-employed have been given a weight of 4 and the rest of the children a weight of unity in the calculations.

The T scores at eight and eleven years are the average of the four tests given at each age. The standard deviations of these average scores are 8·4 at eight and 8·9 at eleven. These, as would be expected, are smaller than those for the individual tests which were designed to have a standard deviation of 10.

* * *

The 'expected' awards of grammar school places are calculated after grouping the children into two regions—those with more than 20 per cent provision of grammar school places and those with less—and two social classes—middle and manual working. Within these four groups divisions are made into ten bands of measured ability. Within each band the children are further subdivided by the levels of a particular factor (e.g. housing, family size). The expected awards within each band of ability are then obtained by multiplying the total number of children at each level of the factor by the proportion of those, at all levels within the band, who were given grammar school places.

Finally, the expected figures are summarised for each factor level over the whole range of measured ability. The total of expected awards, so calculated, is of course equal to the actual awards. A comparison of the observed with expected numbers at each factor level indicates whether and to what extent existing grammar school awards are evenly or unevenly distributed.

When comparing social classes expected figures are calculated in a different way. Here the aim is to show how far grammar school entry in the lower middle and manual working classes falls below that of the upper middle class. At each level of measured ability (at eight or eleven years) the expected awards are obtained by applying the proportion actually given to the upper middle class children, at each level of ability, in turn to the total number of children in each of the other three classes. The total of expected awards is therefore greater than that observed, and the difference between them gives an indication of the number of places that would be needed if all children had the same educational opportunities as upper middle class children judged by their measured ability.

CHAPTER II

SOURCES OF INFORMATION

II(a) Balance Sheet of the Survey (Summer 1957)

	Actual Number of Children	*Percentage of all those living in England and Wales*
Children living in England and Wales:		
Full information[1]	3418 ⎫	81·5 ⎫
Partial information	657 ⎬ 4195[4]	15·7 ⎬ 100%
No educational information[2]	120 ⎭	2·8 ⎭
Children living in Scotland	544	
Children dead or abroad	623	
Total[3]	5362	

[1] Full information = tests completed at eight and eleven years together with details of secondary school allocation.

[2] These children were untraced when the results of the secondary selection examinations were checked with the Local Education Authorities in June 1958.

[3] In 'Children under Five' the total of survey children was 5386, but since then it was discovered that 26 children were illegitimate. Although their parents were living in stable unions it was thought better to exclude them. Two children who were excluded from the earlier report because their forms had been misfiled are included in the present study.

[4] The population estimates are as follows: 8140 children for whom there is full information, 1522 for whom there is partial information and 133 for whom there is no information.

*II(b) Secondary School Allocation of Survey Children in England
and Wales—Distribution of Twelve-Year-Old Children in
Secondary Schools in June 1958[1]*

	National Survey Sample	Ministry of Education[2]
	%	%
Grammar and direct grant schools	19·1	18·3
Secondary modern and selective central schools	63·0	63·9
Independent (whether recognised or not)	5·1	6·3
Technical	2·8	2·0
Special	1·3	1·0
Unallocated or not conventionally streamed	8·7	8·4
Total percentage	100·0	99·9
Number of children	9662[3]	759,719

[1] The final information on secondary school allocation was provided by the Local Education Authorities in June 1958 when the survey children were twelve and a quarter years old.

[2] These figures are derived from the Ministry of Education's report 'Education in 1959' after consultation with the Ministry's Statistical Department.

[3] These and all other numbers given in the following tables are population estimates.

CHAPTER III

SELECTING CHILDREN FOR SECONDARY SCHOOL

III(a) Award of Grammar School Places to Children grouped by Parents' Wishes and their Level of Performance

Test Score at 11 years	Mothers' Wishes		
	Definitely Grammar School	*Doubtful Grammar School*	*Definitely Secondary Modern*
	at Grammar School	at Grammar School	at Grammar School
	%	%	%
49–51	3·9	4·8	nil
52–54	15·8	9·1	3·2
55–57	42·4	21·2	7·7
58–60	61·8	44·0	16·2
61–63	87·4	86·1	52·0
64–66	89·1	91·7	*
67 and over	98·0	83·3	†

* 4 children only, all went to secondary modern schools.
† 1 child only, who went to a grammar school.

CHAPTER IV

REGIONAL INEQUALITIES IN SELECTION

IV(a) Numbers of Children in each Region

Region[1]	Numbers of Children	
	In 1946	In 1957
Wales	527	532
S. West	484	540
N. West	1063	1068
W. & E. Ridings	757	730
East	498	579
N. Midland	731	731
Midlands	865	846
London & S. East	1867	1828
North	814	750
South	495	536
Scotland	39	nil
All children	8140	8140

[1] The regions are listed in order of extent of grammar school provision, from Wales with 28·6% award places to the South with 13·1%.

IV(b) Regional Variations in the Award of Grammar School Places, by those Given and Expected

	Grammar School Places			
		Expected from		
Region in 1957	Awarded	Measured Ability at 11[1]	Teachers' Assess-ment	Mothers' Wishes
	%	%	%	%
Wales	28·6	18·0	43·1	44·9
S. West	26·7	21·1	32·4	32·6
N. West	22·6	21·8	31·4	28·8
W. & E. Ridings	22·0	20·1	33·2	25·0
East	21·0	20·7	31·4	27·5
N. Midland	20·0	19·0	24·8	25·8
Midlands	18·7	19·2	24·9	26·8
London & S. East	18·2	22·3	26·8	31·9
North	17·0	18·6	21·4	25·4
South	13·1	18·0	26·8	26·4

[1] These figures are calculated on the basis of equal regional opportunity for measured ability. They are standardised for social class.

IV(c) Migration—Test Scores of Families who Moved and Stayed Put, by Region

Region	Stayed in Same Region	Moved out of Region	Moved into Region
	Average Test Score at 11	Average Test Score at 11	Average Test Score at 11
Wales	49·35	55·32	51·38
S. West	48·96	54·93	54·05
N. West	51·13	55·25	54·21
W. & E. Ridings	49·82	52·85	55·41
East	50·09	53·23	53·34
N. Midland	49·57	57·34	51·09
Midlands	48·50	52·76	56·56
London & S. East	50·91	52·65	53·87
North	49·68	52·06	50·27
South	49·63	51·77	52·29

IV(d) Moves in the Pre-school Years by Social Class—Average Test Scores

	Middle Class Children	Manual Working Class Children
11-year scores:		
Several moves[1]	54·03	46·99
No moves	54·97	49·18
8-year scores:		
Several moves	52·70	47·08
No moves	54·01	49·85
Numbers of children:		
Several moves	177	472
No moves	702	1817

[1] i.e. more than one move in the pre-school years.

CHAPTER V

THE HOMES

V(a) Standard of Housing by Social Class—Numbers of Children

	Standard of Housing[1]		
Social Class	*Satisfactory*	*Unsatis-factory*	*Incomplete Information*
Middle:			
Upper	470	96	84
Lower	859	626	270
Manual Working:			
Upper	585	989	263
Lower	935	2404	439
Unknown	20	31	69

[1] See definition on page 35.

V(b) Standard of Housing by Social Class—Average Test Scores

Social Class	Age at Test	Standard of Housing		
		Satisfactory	Unsatisfactory	Incomplete Information
Upper Middle:				
	11 years	56·91	56·64	57·88
	8 years	56·79	54·88	57·77
Lower Middle:				
	11 years	55·62	52·08	52·52
	8 years	54·67	51·06	51·90
Upper Manual Working:				
	11 years	52·38	48·91	49·16
	8 years	52·05	49·25	49·15
Lower Manual Working:				
	11 years	50·25	46·66	46·65
	8 years	50·39	47·45	46·34
All Social Classes:				
	11 years	53·40	48·26	49·67
	8 years	53·08	48·61	49·12
Social Class held constant[1]				
	11 years	52·45	49·16	49·41
	8 years	52·22	49·24	48·89

[1] These scores are obtained for each column by weighting the average score in each social class by the proportion in which this class is represented in the whole population. These weighted average scores are then summed to give the figures for 'social class held constant'.

V(c) Standard of Housing by Social Class—Award of Grammar School Places, Comparison of Observed and Expected

Social Class	Standard of Housing	Grammar School Places			
		Awarded	Expected from		
			Measured Ability at 11[1]	Teachers' Assessment	Mothers' Wishes
		%	%	%	%
Middle:					
	Satisfactory	42·5	41·7	59·2	49·9
	Unsatisfactory	27·5	28·9	37·0	41·4
Manual Working:					
	Satisfactory	19·0	18·0	29·0	33·0
	Unsatisfactory	11·4	11·9	17·3	21·5

[1] These figures are calculated on the basis of equal opportunity for measured ability in each type of housing. They are standardised for regional provision of grammar school places.

CHAPTER VI

THE PARENTS

VI(a) Numbers of Children in each Social Class

Social Class	Number of Children
[1]Middle—Upper	650
Lower	1755
Manual Working—Upper	1837
Lower	3778
Unknown	120

VI(b) Home Circumstances of Children by Social Class.

	Middle Class		Manual Working Class	
	Upper	Lower	Upper	Lower
	%	%	%	%
Satisfactory Housing	85·7	61·9	38·1	27·7
Room for Homework	59·4	36·6	30·5	19·2
Television	59·7	64·1	57·6	56·0
Telephone	71·4	38·1	7·6	3·2
Car	59·5	37·9	17·7	11·9

[1] See definition on pages 43 to 45.

VI(c) Primary School by Social Class.

Type of Primary School	Middle Class Children		Manual Working Class Children	
	Upper	*Lower*	*Upper*	*Lower*
	%	%	%	%
Good Academic Record	44·6	29·4	18·2	15·7
Predominantly Middle Class Pupils	68·4	42·8	23·8	16·0
Good Amenities	33·0	25·7	24·1	21·2

VI(d) Social Class—Average Test Scores.

Social Class	Average Test Score at		Change in Score
	11 Years	*8 Years*	
Middle:			
Upper	56·99	56·64	+0·35
Lower	53·88	52·96	+0·92
Manual Working:			
Upper	50·05	49·99	+0·06
Lower	47·55	48·05	—0·50

VI(e) Social Class—Average Scores in each Test.[1]

	Middle Class		Manual Working Class	
	Upper	Lower	Upper	Lower
	Average score	*Average score*	*Average score*	*Average score*
Eight-year tests:				
Picture intelligence	56·13	52·73	50·17	48·82
Reading	56·74	53·45	49·86	47·80
Vocabulary	58·33	53·88	50·19	47·63
Sentence completion	57·30	53·79	49·83	48·02
Eleven-year tests:				
Non-verbal ability	57·03	54·31	50·25	47·99
Verbal ability	57·43	54·32	50·12	47·78
Reading	57·54	54·01	49·89	47·52
Vocabulary	59·18	54·81	50·33	47·36
Arithmetic	57·18	54·43	49·86	47·30

[1] These scores are based on the sample numbers and are *not* population estimates.

VI(f) Social Class by Region—Award of Grammar School Places, Comparison of Observed and Expected.

Social Class	Grammar School Places	Local Education Authorities providing Grammar School Places for	
		more than 20% of children	*20% or less children*
Upper Middle	Number awarded	129	183
	Number expected[1]	128·1	183·8
	Awarded as % of expected	100·6%	99·6%
Lower Middle	Number awarded	303	280
	Number expected	305·6	387·6
	Awarded as % of expected	99·1%	72·2%
Upper manual working	Number awarded	171	158
	Number expected	201·5	265·2
	Awarded as % of expected	84·9%	59·6%
Lower manual working	Number awarded	216	193
	Number expected	301·6	368·7
	Awarded as % of expected	71·6%	52·3%

[1] Expected if at each level of measured ability at eleven years they had the same chance of going to grammar schools as upper middle class children of similar ability.

VI(g) Social Class—Award of Grammar School Places, Comparison of Observed and Expected.

| Social Class | Grammar School Places | | | Teachers' Assessment | Mothers' Wishes |
| | Awarded | Expected if same chances as upper middle at each level of score at | | | |
		11 years	8 years		
	%	%	%	%	%
Middle:					
Upper	54·3	54·3	54·3	66·7	57·2
Lower	34·0	40·4	41·5	45·2	44·1
Manual Working:					
Upper	18·1	25·7	31·7	27·7	29·8
Lower	11·0	18·1	25·7	16·7	22·4

CHAPTER VII

PARENTAL ENCOURAGEMENT

VII(a) Parents' Attitudes to Education by Social Class—Number of children.

Social Class	Level of Interest[1]			
	High	Average	Low	Unknown
Middle:				
Upper	242	197	167	44
Lower	328	443	911	73
Manual Working:				
Upper	193	414	1189	41
Lower	182	627	2842	127
Unknown	5	26	88	1

[1] See definitions on page 54.

VII(b) Parents' Attitudes to Education by Social Class—Average Test Scores.

Social Class	Age at Test	Level of Interest			
		High	Average	Low	Unknown
		Average score	*Average score*	*Average score*	*Average score*
Upper Middle	11 years	59·26	55·65	55·60	55·80
	8 years	58·29	56·14	54·84	56·59
Lower Middle	11 years	58·60	54·85	51·64	54·73
	8 years	56·98	53·62	51·00	55·29
Upper Manual Working	11 years	54·73	52·42	48·58	46·80
	8 years	54·22	52.00	48·73	46·07
Lower Manual Working	11 years	55·38	50·20	46·39	49·26
	8 years	54·30	50·27	47·12	48·85
All Social Classes	11 years	57·36	52·61	48·14	51·32
	8 years	56·23	52·27	48·44	51·29
Social Class held constant[1]	11 years	56·25	52·16	48·78	50·41
	8 years	55·19	51·87	48·96	50·24

[1] See note to Table V(b).

VII(c) Parents' Attitudes to Education—Average Scores in each Test.[1]

| | Level of Interest | | |
| | High | Average | Low |
	Average score	Average score	Average score
Eight-year tests:			
Picture Intelligence	54·30	52·04	49·52
Reading	56·16	51·85	48·63
Vocabulary	55·84	52·12	49·00
Sentence completion	56·61	52·20	48·82
Eleven-year tests:			
Non-verbal ability	55·64	52·32	49·27
Verbal ability	56·42	52·38	48·98
Reading	56·44	52·42	48·56
Vocabulary	56·82	52·87	48·84
Arithmetic	56·74	52·23	48·51

[1] These scores are based on the sample numbers and are *not* population estimates. Social class is held constant.

VII(d) Parents' Attitudes to Education by Social Class—Award of Grammar School Places, Comparison of Observed and Expected.

Social Class	Level of Parents' Interest	Grammar School Places			
		Awarded	Expected from		
			Measured Ability at 11[1]	Teachers' Comments	Mothers' Wishes
		%	%	%	%
Middle	High	57·2	53·9	79·3	67·7
	Average	40·1	38·4	53·7	47·0
	Low	24·8	27·6	34·1	37·1
Manual Working	High	40·5	34·3	58·8	48·5
	Average	16·9	17·5	26·5	29·7
	Low	9·6	10·1	14·9	21·1

VII(e) Parents' Attitudes to Education—Award of Grammar School Places to Children scoring between 55 and 60 in Eleven-year Tests.

Level of Parents' Interest	Grammar School Places	
	Awarded	Expected[2]
	%	%
High	46·2	38·7
Average	41·4	37·9
Low	30·1	34·9

[1] These figures are calculated on the basis of equal opportunity for measured ability in each type of family. They are standardised for regional provision of grammar school places.

[2] After allowing for social class and regional differences in the award of grammar school places.

CHAPTER VIII

CHILDREN'S ATTITUDES AND BEHAVIOUR

VIII(a) Parents' and Children's Attitudes Compared.

Level of Parents' Interest	Children's Attitude to Work			
	Hard or Very Hard Worker	*Average Worker*	*Poor Worker or Lazy*	*Total %*
High %	69·5	26·8	3·7	100·0
Average %	47·3	42·1	10·6	100·0
Low %	32·6	48·4	19·0	100·0

VIII(b) Teachers' Assessment of Attitude to Work by Social Class —Numbers of Children.

Social Class	Children's Attitude to Work					
	Very Hard Worker	*Hard Worker*	*Average Worker*	*Poor Worker*	*Lazy*	*Not assessed*
Middle						
Upper	154	166	217	36	16	61
Lower	281	522	664	147	35	106
Manual Working						
Upper	192	440	845	226	53	81
Lower	264	884	1672	590	161	207
Unknown	9	26	52	9	7	17

VIII(c) Teachers' Assessment of Attitude to Work by Social Class—Average Test Scores.

Social Class	Age at Test	Children's Attitude to Work					
		Very Hard Worker	*Hard Worker*	*Average Worker*	*Poor Worker*	*Lazy*	*Not Assessed*
Upper Middle	11 years	62·91	57·72	54·62	48·53	51·44	55·00
	8 years	60·46	57·07	55·21	51·56	49·94	55·64
Lower Middle	11 years	59·96	56·20	52·16	43·15	47·68	54·09
	8 years	58·20	54·84	51·17	44·34	48·91	54·23
Upper Manual Working	11 years	58·47	53·81	49·10	40·93	45·55	48·09
	8 years	56·60	52·74	49·13	43·82	47·26	47·27
Lower Manual Working	11 years	57·67	50·81	46·89	41·31	42·73	47·62
	8 years	56·25	50·28	47·66	43·28	45·04	47·12
All Social Classes	11 years	59·47	53·43	48·96	41·75	44·48	50·20
	8 years	57·67	52·56	49·20	43·86	46·29	49·95
Social Class held constant[1]	11 years	58·77	53·23	49·17	42·20	45·16	49·74
	8 years	57·09	52·39	49·37	44·28	46·79	49·39

[1] See note to Table V(b).

VIII(d) Teachers' Assessment of Attitude to Work by Social Class—Award of Grammar School Places, Comparison of Observed and Expected.

| | | Grammar School Places | | | |
| | | | Expected from | | |
Social Class	Children's Attitude to Work	Awarded	Measured Ability at 11[1]	Teachers' Comments	Mothers' Wishes
		%	%	%	%
Middle	Hard or Very Hard Worker	55·4	51·3	76·7	55·3
	Average or Poor Worker	18·3	22·5	24·5	39·7
Manual Working	Hard or Very Hard Worker	30·2	26·0	46·7	33·0
	Average or Poor Worker	4·5	6·6	6·5	20·6

[1] These figures are calculated on the basis of equal opportunity for measured ability in each group of children. They are standardised for regional provision of grammar school places.

VIII(e) Children's Attitude to Work by Measured Ability—Award of Grammar School Places.

Score at 11 years	Children's Attitude to Work		
	Very Hard Worker at Grammar School	Hard Worker at Grammar School	Average, Poor Worker, or Lazy at Grammar School
	%	%	%
49–51	11·1	4·7	2·3
52–54	16·9	11·9	6·0
55–57	31·7	35·1	19·1
58–60	62·7	53·6	35·5
61–63	95·0	88·3	66·0
64–66	89·5	80·7	75·6
67 and over	92·1	95·5	78·3

VIII(f) Symptoms of Disturbed Behaviour by Social Class—Numbers of Children.

Social Class	Number of Symptoms of Disturbed Behaviour				
	None	One	Two	Three or Four	Un-known
Middle:					
Upper	283	227	76	15	49
Lower	832	631	176	37	79
Manual Working:					
Upper	769	705	216	46	101
Lower	1758	1322	472	61	165
Unknown	58	31	23	0	8

VIII(g) Symptoms of Disturbed Behaviour by Social Class—Average Test Score.

Social Class	Age at Test	Number of Symptoms of Disturbed Behaviour				
		None	*One*	*Two*	*Three or Four*	*Un-known*
Upper Middle	11 years	57·53	56·96	55·67	52·53	57·45
	8 years	56·36	56·49	57·55	52·73	58·69
Lower Middle	11 years	53·84	54·25	53·06	52·19	53·91
	8 years	52·73	53·47	52·51	52·41	52·53
Upper Manual Working	11 years	50·77	50·47	48·80	43·89	47·11
	8 years	50·17	50·84	48·93	45·39	46·92
Lower Manual Working	11 years	47·74	47·57	47·00	44·49	48·10
	8 years	48·26	47·83	48·26	47·02	47·35
All Social Classes	11 years	50·53	50·48	49·24	46·87	50·18
	8 years	50·31	50·48	49·96	48·34	49·69
Social Class held constant[1]	11 years	50·55	50·45	49·43	46·68	49·89
	8 years	50·33	50·45	50·09	48·28	49·29

[1] See note to Table V(b).

CHAPTER IX

BOYS AND GIRLS

IX(a) Boys and Girls by Social Class—Award of Grammar School Places, Comparison of Observed and Expected.

Social Class	Sex	Grammar School Places			
		Awarded	Expected from		
			Measured Ability at 11[1]	Teachers' Comments	Mothers' Wishes
		%	%	%	%
Middle:					
	Boys	32·9	36·4	45·4	46·9
	Girls	42·2	38·2	57·0	48·2
Manual Working:					
	Boys	13·0	12·6	17·0	23·4
	Girls	13·1	13·6	23·6	26·2

[1] These figures are calculated on the basis of equal opportunity for measured ability in each group of children. They are standardised for regional provision of grammar school places.

CHAPTER X

EARLY ADOLESCENCE
(Girls Only)

X(a) Age of Puberty by Social Class.

Social Class	Age at First Period[1]			Total %	Number of Girls
	Early	Average	Late		
Middle:					
Upper %	35·5	32·5	32·0	100·0	200
Lower %	40·5	35·9	23·6	100·0	424
Manual Working					
Upper %	39·7	32·5	27·8	100·0	277
Lower %	39·0	31·7	29·3	100·0	526
All girls	39·1	33·2	27·7	100·0	1427

X(b) Age of Puberty by Completed Family Size.

Completed Family Size	Age at First Period[2]			Total %	Number of Girls
	Early %	Average %	Late %		
One	53·0	28·3	18·7	100·0	219
Two	39·2	36·1	24·7	100·0	502
Three	36·0	33·6	30·4	100·0	342
4 or more	33·5	31·9	34·6	100·0	364

[1] These figures are based on the sample numbers and are *not* population estimates. See definition on page 78.

[2] These figures are based on the sample numbers and are *not* population estimates.

CHAPTER XI

FIRST AND LATER BORN

XI(a) Position in Family by Social Class—Numbers of Children

Social Class	Only Child	Two-Child Families		Three-Child Families		
		Elder	Younger	Eldest	Middle	Youngest
Middle:						
Upper	72	138	147	62	62	69
Lower	310	326	382	110	137	136
Manual Working:						
Upper	262	299	280	125	171	142
Lower	455	479	574	197	272	335
Unknown	26	8	14	13	6	3

XI(b) Position in Family by Social Class—Average Test Scores.

Social Class	Age at Test	Only Child	Two-Child Families		Three-Child Families		
			Elder	Younger	Eldest	Middle	Youngest
Upper	11 years	59·85	57·21	57·47	57·71	55·92	54·20
Middle	8 years	59·21	56·50	57·24	56·90	56·53	53·61
Lower	11 years	54·50	55·01	55·49	54·40	52·15	53·02
Middle	8 years	53·77	53·82	54·59	53·28	51·82	52·34
Upper Manual	11 years	52·74	52·36	51·98	50·34	49·55	49·56
	8 years	52·27	51·66	51·62	49·54	49·93	49·87
Lower Manual Working	11 years	51·03	49·65	47·86	47·48	48·38	48·63
	8 years	51·56	50·02	49·26	47·59	47·91	49·51
All Social Classes	11 years	52·99	52·55	51·82	51·03	50·22	50·26
	8 years	52·85	52·13	52·06	50·52	50·12	50·57
Social Class held constant[1]	11 years	52·88	52·05	51·25	50·47	50·08	50·25
	8 years	52·82	51·75	51·61	50·02	49·92	50·54

[1] See Table V(b).

CHAPTER XII

COMPLETED FAMILY SIZE

XII(a) Completed Family Size by Social Class—Numbers of Children.

Social Class	Completed Family Size							
	One	*Two*	*Three*	*Four*	*Five*	*Six*	*Seven or More*	*Un-known*
Middle:								
Upper	72	285	193	68	20	7	3	2
Lower	310	708	383	174	93	46	38	3
Manual working								
Upper	262	579	438	283	136	53	78	8
Lower	455	1053	804	617	329	202	296	22
Unknown	26	22	22	12	8	2	8	20

XII(b) Completed Family Size by Social Class—Average Test Scores.

Social Class	Age at Test	Completed Family Size							
		One	Two	Three	Four	Five	Six	Seven or More	Un-known
Upper Middle	11 years	59·87	57·31	55·80	56·49	55·65	54·45	54·00	55·00
	8 years	59·20	56·82	55·44	56·79	54·60	52·14	54·33	63·50
Lower Middle	11 years	54·60	55·27	53·20	52·02	51·81	50·11	47·81	59·00
	8 years	53·88	54·26	52·64	50·20	50·03	51·43	47·95	58·00
Upper Manual Working	11 years	52·74	52·19	49·90	48·61	47·40	45·80	40·54	47·50
	8 years	52·27	51·64	49·93	48·65	47·31	48·53	42·49	44·00
Lower Manual Working	11 years	50·93	48·71	48·16	46·64	45·78	44·86	42·19	44·73
	8 years	51·54	49·64	48·38	47·44	45·27	45·51	42·44	45·09
All Social Classes	11 years	52·96	52·16	50·41	48·57	47·51	46·04	42·49	47·17
	8 years	52·86	52·09	50·36	48·74	46·87	47·07	43·06	47·00
Social Class held constant[1]	11 years	52·87	51·63	50·27	49·06	48·26	46·97	43·98	49·31
	8 years	52·83	51·69	50·23	49·07	47·53	48·03	44·61	49·14

[1] See Table V(b).

XII(c) Completed Family Size by Father's Age at Birth of Survey Child—Average Test Score.[1]

	Completed Family Size			
	One	*Two*	*Three*	*Four or More*
Age of Father	*Average Test Score at 11*	*Average Test Score at 11*	*Average Test Score at 11*	*Average Test Score at 11*
Under 30	52·78	52·25	50·35	48·11
30–34	53·03	50·94	50·18	47·61
35 and over	54·38	52·54	51·46	47·72

XII(d) Completed Family Size by Social Class—Award of Grammar School Places, Comparison of Observed and Expected.

		Grammar School Places			
			Expected from		
Social Class	*Completed Family Size*	*Awarded*	*Measured ability at 11*[2]	*Teachers' Comments*	*Mothers' Wishes*
		%	%	%	%
Middle	1 or 2	41·8	41·8	56·9	48·5
	3	38·6	33·9	50·0	49·6
	4 or more	21·9	27·7	33·4	42·0
Manual working	1 or 2	18·0	17·0	27·2	32·1
	3	13·2	14·1	22·4	24·2
	4 or more	7·2	7·9	10·6	16·3

[1] These scores are based on the sample numbers and are *not* population estimates. Social class is held constant.

[2] These figures are calculated on the basis of equal opportunity for measured ability in each group of children. They are standardised for regional provision of grammar school places.

*XII(e) Family Size by Social Class—Mothers' Attitudes and
Interests.*[1]

	Middle Class				Manual Working Class			
	Completed Family Size				Completed Family Size			
	One	Two	Three	Four or More	One	Two	Three	Four or More
	%	%	%	%	%	%	%	%
Good Infant Care	58·4	46·5	36·6	27·8	37·1	23·5	16·0	5·9
Good Infant Management	60·5	53·5	56·1	52·2	37·7	36·2	34·1	20·5
Good Use of Medical Services	78·6	79·4	67·2	51·2	63·3	55·8	47·9	30·9
High Interest in School Progress	31·5	30·7	28·5	18·7	15·0	10·6	6·6	1·8
Desires Grammar School Place[2]	74·8	76·2	71·9	62·1	69·0	59·1	50·3	40·3
Late School Leaving Wished	53·0	56·3	55·9	43·2	27·2	21·7	15·2	7·9
At least 4 of the above	76·2	71·5	63·1	47·0	45·6	35·9	23·8	8·2

[1] These figures are based on the sample numbers and are *not* population estimates.
[2] Irrespective of leaving age desired.

CHAPTER XIII

THE PRIMARY SCHOOLS

XIII(a) Academic Record of Primary Schools by Social Class—
Numbers of Children.

Social Class	Academic Record of Primary Schools[1]			
	Good	Fair	Poor	Unknown
Middle:				
Upper	260	275	60	55
Lower	470	868	331	86
Manual Working:				
Upper	327	1014	405	91
Lower	547	2028	1014	189
Unknown	17	73	25	5

[1] See definitions on page 104

XIII(b) Academic Record of Primary Schools by Social Class Average Test Scores.

Social Class	Age at Test	Academic Record of Primary School			
		Good	Fair	Poor	Unknown
Upper Middle	11 years	58·41	56·83	53·57	54·86
	8 years	57·19	56·15	55·33	57·91
Lower Middle	11 years	57·02	53·52	51·23	50·61
	8 years	55·29	52·60	51·18	50·62
Upper Manual Working	11 years	52·85	50·09	47·86	49·28
	8 years	52·12	50·07	48·47	48·13
Lower Manual Working	11 years	49·08	48·06	46·19	45·03
	8 years	49·10	48·46	46·94	46·60
All Social Classes	11 years	53·69	50·26	47·73	48·37
	8 years	52·84	50·21	48·34	49·23
Social Class held constant[1]	11 years	52·43	50·42	48·27	48·02
	8 years	51·80	50·35	48·89	48·74

[1] See Table V(b).

XIII(c) *Academic Record of Primary Schools—Average Scores in each Test.*[1]

Tests	Academic Record of Primary School		
	Good	Fair	Poor
	Average Score	Average Score	Average Score
Eight-year tests:			
Picture intelligence	51·70	50·59	49·73
Reading	51·89	50·17	48·80
Vocabulary	52·05	50·43	48·84
Sentence completion	52·15	50·46	48·87
Eleven-year tests:			
Non-verbal ability	52·06	50·83	48·85
Verbal ability	52·91	50·56	48·75
Reading	52·21	50·17	48·67
Vocabulary	52·48	50·69	48·56
Arithmetic	53·06	50·18	47·61

[1] These scores are based on the sample numbers and are *not* population estimates. Social class is held constant.

XIII(d) *Academic Record of Primary Schools by Social Class—*
Award of Grammar School Places, Comparison of Observed
and Expected.

Social Class	Academic Record of Primary School	Grammar School Places			
		Awarded	Expected from		
			Measured Ability at 11[1]	Teachers' Comments	Mothers' Wishes
Middle:		%	%	%	%
	Good	53·2	48·0	61·2	57·7
	Fair	35·5	34·8	49·2	46·9
	Poor	14·6	23·0	39·4	36·1
Manual Working:					
	Good	26·8	19·6	32·3	30·6
	Fair	13·3	14·0	20·0	26·6
	Poor	4·8	7·8	14·8	17·9

[1] These figures are calculated on the basis of equal opportunity for measured ability in each group of children. They are standardised for regional provision of grammar school places.

XIII(e) Academic Record of Primary Schools by Regional Provision of Grammar School Places and Measured Ability— Percentage going to Grammar Schools.

	Regions where Grammar School Places are provided for more than 20% of children			Regions where Grammar School Places are provided for 20% or less of children		
Test Score at Eleven Years	Academic Record of Primary School			Academic Record of Primary School		
	Good	Average	Poor	Good	Average	Poor
	% to Grammar Schools	% to Grammar Schools	% to Grammar Schools	% to Grammar Schools	% to Grammar Schools	% to Grammar Schools
49–54	13·7	7·3	3·0	9·4	3·3	3·9
55–57	60·8	32·1	20·4	32·2	17·7	5·9
58–60	67·8	53·9	25·6	55·6	44·6	19·4
61–63	97·6	92·1	64·3	90·8	77·0	61·8
64–66	100·0	93·2	*	78·2	81·2	72·7
67–99	100·0	78·9	*	87·8	97·3	*

* Less than twenty children.

CHAPTER XIV

STREAMING BY ABILITY

XIV(a) Streaming by Ability—Distribution of Eight-year Test Scores.

Test Scores at 8 Years	Streams	
	Upper	Lower
	Numbers of Children	Numbers of Children
32—	0	17
34—	0	17
36—	0	20
38—	0	31
40—	9	44
42—	9	59
44—	21	59
46—	43	70
48—	64	37
50—	73	26
52—	77	28
54—	88	11
56—	69	10
58—	60	11
60—	69	4
62—	50	0
64—	47	0
66—	17	0
68—	16	0
70—	3	0
72—	0	0
74—	1	0
76—	4	0
78 and over	1	0
Total	721	444

XIV(b) Streaming by Ability by Level of Test Score at Eight—Changes in Score.

Test Score at 8 years	2-stream schools Change in Test Score	1-stream schools Change in Test Score	Difference (2-stream minus 1-stream schools)
0–34	+4·40	+0·50	+3·90
35–40	+1·69	+1·28	+0·41
41–45	+0·96	+0·77	+0·19
46–48	+1·51	+0·97	+0·54
49–51	+2·67	+0·09	+2·58
52–54	+0·26	−0·18	+0·44
55–57	+1·77	−1·27	+3·04
58–60	+0·02	−0·25	+0·27
61–63	−0·27	−1·18	+0·91
64–66	−0·83	−2·26	−0·57
67–69	−3·67	−4·63	+0·96
70 and over	−8·87	−6·67	−2·20

(+ = improved   − = deteriorated)

CHAPTER XV

WASTE OF ABILITY

XV(a) Social Class by Level of Ability at Eight and Eleven—
Percentage of Fifteen-year-old Children attending Grammar
Schools.

(i) *Grouped by Eight Year Ability*

| Test Score at 8 years | Middle Class | | Manual Working Class | |
| | Upper | Lower | Upper | Lower |
	At Grammar School	At Grammar School	At Grammar School	At Grammar School
	%	%	%	%
49–51	23·2	13·2	7·0	10·0
52–54	52·8	36·2	18·4	14·7
55–57	58·2	48·6	30·7	29·0
58–60	72·8	62·8	46·8	34·7
61–63	81·2	70·8	67·3	53·0
64–66	86·2	85·1	88·6	52·5
67 and over	86·8	91·0	78·4	82·9

(ii) Grouped by Eleven Year Ability

	Middle Class		Manual Working Class	
	Upper	Lower	Upper	Lower
Test Score at 11 years	At Grammar School	At Grammar School	At Grammar School	At Grammar School
	%	%	%	%
49–51	16·7	2·5	3·3	3·5
52–54	27·4	18·4	13·1	7·2
55–57	59·3	39·0	25·0	26·6
58–60	63·3	59·7	46·1	51·8
61–63	94·0	86·5	97·9	79·7
64–66	94·0	87·7	80·0	89·0
67 and over	100·0	92·9	97·8	100·0

XV(b) Social Class by Level of Ability at Eleven—Percentage of Fifteen-year-old Children attending Grammar or Technical Schools.

	Middle Class		Manual Working Class	
	Upper	Lower	Upper	Lower
Test Score at 11 years	At Grammar or Technical Schools	At Grammar or Technical Schools	At Grammar or Technical Schools	At Grammar or Technical Schools
	%	%	%	%
49–51	16·7	10·5	7·1	6·1
52–54	29·0	28·7	23·4	14·3
55–57	69·8	52·7	39·3	42·5
58–60	65·8	74·6	56·1	65·8
61–63	97·6	91·6	99·0	86·2
64–66	94·0	92·4	88·9	100·0
67 and over	100·0	98·8	97·8	100·0

XV(c) Social Class by Level of Ability at Eleven—Percentage of Fifteen-year-old Children attending Grammar, Technical or Independent Schools.

| | Middle Class | | Manual Working Class | |
| | Upper | Lower | Upper | Lower |
Test Score at 11 years	At Grammar, Technical, or Independent Schools	At Grammar, Technical, or Independent Schools	At Grammar, Technical, or Independent Schools	At Grammar, Technical, or Independent Schools
	%	%	%	%
43–45	42·9	5·6	3·7	1·4
46–48	43·6	5·6	5·4	4·4
49–51	31·0	14·8	7·1	7·1
52–54	43·6	34·1	23·4	16·3
55–57	79·1	56·4	42·9	43·6
58–60	81·2	78·6	58·3	65·8
61–63	97·6	93·5	99·0	86·2
64–66	100·0	92·4	88·9	100·0
67 and over	100·0	98·8	97·8	100·0

BIBLIOGRAPHY

Volume numbers of journals are in bold type and page numbers
in ordinary type

ABERNETHY, E. M. *Relationships Between Mental and Physical Growth*. Monograph of the Society for Research in Child Development. (1936), **1**, No. 7.

BOARD OF EDUCATION. *Educational Reconstruction*. Her Majesty's Stationery Office, Cmd.6458. (1943).

CROWTHER, G. (Report) *15* to *18*. Ministry of Education Central Advisory Council for Education. Her Majesty's Stationery Office (1959).

DANIELS, J. C. Effects of Streaming in the Primary School. *British Journal of Educational Psychology* (1961), **31**, 69, 119.

DAVIS, A. *Social Class Influences Upon Learning*. Cambridge: Harvard University Press (1948).

DAVIS, A. *Intelligence and Cultural Differences*. University of Chicago Press (1951).

FLOUD, J. E., and HALSEY, A. H. Intelligence Tests, Social Class and Selection for Secondary Schools. *British Journal of Sociology* (1957), **8**, 33.

FLOUD, J. E., HALSEY, A. H., and MARTIN, F. M. *Social Class and Educational Opportunity*. Heinemann (1957).

GALTON, F. *English Men of Science*. Macmillan (1874).

GILDEA, M. C. L., DOMKE, H. R., MENSH, I. N., BUCHMUELLER, A. D., GLIDEWELL, J. C., and KANTOR, M. B. Community Mental Health Research— Findings after three years. *American Journal of Psychiatry* (1958), **114**, 970.

GLASS, R. *The Social Background of a Plan—A Study of Middlesbrough*. Routledge & Kegan Paul (1948).

GOLDBERG, M. L., JUSTMAN, J., PASSOW, A. H., and HAGE, G. *The Effects of Ability Grouping*. Horace Mann– Lincoln Institute of School Experimentation. Teachers College, Columbia University (1961).

HOGBEN, L. *Political Arithmetic*. Allen & Unwin (1938).

HSIAO, H. H. The Status of the First Born with Special Reference to Intelligence. *Genetic Psychology Monographs* (1931), **9**, No. 1–2.

JORDAN, A. M. Parental Occupations and Children's Intelligence Scores. *Journal of Applied Psychology* (1933), **17**, 103.

KOCH, H. L. Relation of 'Primary Mental Abilities' in Five and Six Year Olds and Sex of Child and Characteristics of his Siblings. *Child Development* (1954), **25**, 209.

LONDON COUNTY COUNCIL. *Report on the Heights and Weights of School Pupils* (1961).

MACPHERSON, J. *Eleven Year Olds Grow Up*. University of London Press (1958).

MARSHALL, T. H. *Citizenship and Social Class*. Cambridge University Press (1950).

MAXWELL, J. *Social Implications of the 1947 Scottish Mental Survey*. University of London Press (1953).

MAXWELL, J. *The Level and Trend of National Intelligence*. University of London Press (1961).

MORRIS, J. M. *Reading in the Primary School*. National Foundation for Educational Research in England and Wales. Publication No. 12. Newnes (1959).

NEFF, W. S. Socio-Economic Status and Intelligence. *Psychological Bulletin* (1938), **35**, 727.

RUSSELL, W. R. *Physiology of Learning*. Edinburgh Royal College of Physicians (1957).

SCOTTISH COUNCIL FOR RESEARCH IN EDUCATION. *The Trend of Scottish Intelligence*. University of London Press (1949).

SPENS, W. *Secondary Education*. Her Majesty's Stationery Office (1938).

STECKEL, M. L. Intelligence and Birth Order in Family. *Journal of Social Psychology* (1930), **1**, 329.

STROUD, J. B., and LINDQUIST, E. F. Sex Differences and Achievement in the Elementary and Secondary Schools. *Journal of Educational Psychology* (1942), **33**, 657.

TANNER, J. M. *Growth at Adolescence*. Oxford: Blackwell (1955).

THOMSON, G. H. The Northumberland Mental Tests. *British Journal of Psychology* (1921), **12**, 201.

THURSTONE, L. L., and JENKINS, R. L. Birth Order and Intelligence. *Journal of Educational Psychology* (1929), **20**, 641.

THURSTONE, L. L., and JENKINS, R. L. *Order of Birth, Parent-age and Intelligence.* University of Chicago Press (1931).

UNDERWOOD COMMITTEE. *Report of the Committee on Maladjusted Children.* Her Majesty's Stationery Office. (1955).

YATES, A., and PIDGEON, D. A. Transfer at 11+. *Educational Research* (1958), **1**, 13.

YATES, A., and PIDGEON, D. A. *Admission to Grammar Schools.* Newnes (1957).

MEMBERS OF THE JOINT COMMITTEE

OF THE

INSTITUTE OF CHILD HEALTH (UNIVERSITY OF LONDON)
SOCIETY OF MEDICAL OFFICERS OF HEALTH
POPULATION INVESTIGATION COMMITTEE

Chairman: The late Professor James Young
Vice-Chairman: Professor A. A. Moncrieff
Secretary: Professor D. V. Glass
Director: Dr J. W. B. Douglas
Research Officer: Mrs J. M. Clow

Dr Cecile Asher
Professor J. H. F. Brotherston
N. H. Carrier, Esq.
Dr H. M. Cohen
Mrs D. L. Covington
Sir Allen Daley
Dr Mary L. Gilchrist
Professor E. Grebenik
Professor Sir Aubrey Lewis
Dr D. MacCarthy
Dr Jean M. Mackintosh
Miss M. T. McBride
Dr F. J. W. Miller
Dr A. P. Norman
Dr Elfed Thomas
Professor R. M. Titmuss
Dr J. Tizard
Dr W. D. Wall
Dr F. Yates

INDEX